Financial Literacy XL

Curriculum For Financial Education

Published by PWR Publishing LLC

Printed in the United States of America

ISBN: 978-1-7330206-3-3

Contents

How to Create a Budget

At 23, Mathew found himself overwhelmed by his finances. He had a steady job, but his bank account never seemed to reflect his hard work. Between rent, student loans, and impulse spending on takeout and gadgets, he was living paycheck to paycheck. After realizing he had no savings and was starting to accumulate credit card debt, Mathew knew something had to change.

One evening, after another frustrating look at his bank statement, he decided to take control. He spent hours reading articles and watching videos about budgeting, and finally, he created his first budget.

Mathew's budget was simple but effective:

- **Income**: He listed his monthly take-home pay.
- **Fixed expenses**: Rent, utilities, student loans—he couldn't change these, but at least he could account for them.
- **Variable expenses**: Groceries, entertainment, dining out—this was where Mathew saw room for improvement.
- **Savings goals**: He set aside a small portion of his income for an emergency fund and future investments.

To track his spending, Mathew downloaded a budgeting app and categorized every purchase. At first, it was difficult to stick to his new limits. He missed the convenience of ordering takeout and found himself tempted to splurge on things he didn't need. But after the first month, he saw a difference. He had money left over—something that hadn't happened in years.

Over the next few months, Mathew became more disciplined. He found cheaper ways to have fun, like cooking meals at home with friends or exploring free local events. Slowly, his savings grew, and the burden of debt began to shrink. He even started a small investment account, something he had always thought was out of reach.

A year later, Mathew looked back on his progress with pride. He was no longer stressed about money. He had a growing emergency fund, was making extra payments on his student loans, and had built healthy spending habits. The simple act of creating a budget had completely transformed his financial direction.

Mathew realized that taking control of his finances didn't require a huge salary or drastic lifestyle changes—it just required discipline, planning, and commitment to a budget. Now, he felt prepared for whatever financial challenges or opportunities lay ahead.

In today's inflation crisis, creating a budget is a crucial step in managing your finances and achieving your financial goals. Here's a step-by-step guide on how to create an effective budget that you can use to help you build wealth, protect wealth and preserve wealth.

1. Track Your Income

Identify Your Total Income: Start by calculating your total monthly income. This includes your salary, wages, freelance income, rental income, or any other regular sources of income.

Net Income: Use your net income (after taxes) to ensure you're budgeting based on the actual amount you have to spend.

2. List Your Expenses

Fixed Expenses: These are consistent monthly payments like rent/mortgage, utilities, insurance, loan payments, and subscriptions.

Variable Expenses: These are fluctuating expenses such as groceries, transportation, entertainment, and dining out. Estimate based on past spending.

Irregular or Annual Expenses: Plan for periodic expenses like annual subscriptions, insurance premiums, holiday gifts, or car repairs by dividing these costs over the year.

3. Categorize Your Expenses

Break your expenses into key categories, such as:

Housing: Rent, mortgage, utilities, etc.

Transportation: Fuel, public transportation, car maintenance, etc.

Food: Groceries, dining out, etc.

Savings: Emergency fund, retirement savings, etc.

Debt Repayment: Credit card bills, student loans, etc.

Entertainment & Miscellaneous: Hobbies, streaming services, etc.

This will give you a clear picture of where your money is going.

4. Set Financial Goals

Identify short-term goals (like saving for a vacation or paying off debt) and long-term goals (like buying a home or saving for retirement).

Allocate a portion of your budget toward reaching these goals, such as saving a fixed percentage of your income.

5. Compare Income vs. Expenses

Calculate Your Cash Flow: Subtract your total expenses from your total income. If you have money left over, you have a positive cash flow; if expenses exceed income, you have a negative cash flow.

Adjust If Necessary: If you're spending more than you're earning, identify areas where you can cut back on variable or discretionary expenses.

6. Allocate for Savings and Debt Repayment

Aim to save at least 20% of your income if possible. You can split this into an emergency fund, retirement savings, and other financial goals.

Prioritize debt repayment to avoid high-interest costs. Focus on paying off high-interest debt first while making minimum payments on others.

7. Create an Emergency Fund

Set aside funds for emergencies (e.g., unexpected medical bills, car repairs). Aim to build an emergency fund covering 3-6 months' worth of living expenses.

8. Monitor and Adjust Regularly

Track Your Spending: Use budgeting apps or a simple spreadsheet to track your actual spending against your budget.

Review Your Budget Monthly: Compare your actual income and expenses with your budget. Adjust your budget if necessary based on new financial circumstances or unexpected expenses.

9. Automate Your Savings

Set up automatic transfers to your savings or retirement accounts. This way, saving becomes a regular habit without requiring manual effort.

10. Be Flexible

A budget should be flexible. Life changes, and so do your financial needs. Adjust your budget to accommodate changes in income, expenses, or financial goals.

Quiz

1. What key changes did Mathew make to his spending habits that allowed him to save money over the course of a year?

   ____

   ____

2. How did Mathew use his budget to prioritize both paying down debt and building an emergency fund?

   ____

   ____

3. What tools or strategies did Mathew use to track his expenses and stay disciplined with his budget for a full year?

   ____

   ____

How to create a One-year plan

Abigale felt like she was stuck in a financial rut. She had a stable job, but her savings were minimal, and unexpected expenses always seemed to drain her paycheck. She just turned 42 and a single mother of two kids in middle school and retirement looming closer, she realized that if she didn't take control now, her financial future might not be as secure as she hoped.

One evening, after talking with a friend about goal-setting, Abigale decided to take action. She sat down at her kitchen table with a notebook and created a one-year plan for her finances.

Step 1: Define Her Goals Abigale listed her top three financial priorities for the next year:

Build an emergency fund with three months of living expenses.

Pay off her remaining credit card debt.

Start contributing to her retirement fund more aggressively.

Step 2: Break Down Each Goal She broke each goal into smaller, manageable steps:

For the emergency fund, she committed to setting aside a portion of her paycheck each month.

For the credit card debt, she created a payment plan, starting with the smallest balance to gain momentum.

For retirement savings, she decided to cut unnecessary expenses and contribute an additional 5% to her 401(k) every month.

Step 3: Create a Monthly Budget Abigale built a budget that reflected her new priorities. She tracked every dollar, cutting back on dining out, canceling unused subscriptions, and selling a few items she no longer needed. Every extra bit of cash went toward her goals.

Step 4: Stay Accountable To stay on track, Abigale used a financial planner to track her progress each month. She also shared her plan with a close friend, who checked in with her regularly to offer encouragement and celebrate small wins.

One Year Later By the end of the year, Abigale's financial situation had completely transformed. She had saved enough to fully fund her emergency account, leaving her with peace of mind. Her credit card debt was wiped out, and she no longer worried about high-interest payments hanging over her. Best of all, her increased retirement contributions had her feeling more confident about her future.

Reflecting on her journey, Abigale realized that the one-year plan had not only changed her finances but also her mindset. She felt empowered, in control, and capable of achieving even bigger goals. By breaking her goals into actionable steps and staying disciplined, she had shifted the financial direction of her life, ensuring a more secure future for herself and her family.

It was once said that creating a one-year plan is an effective way to set goals, stay focused, and make measurable progress over a defined period. Here's a step-by-step guide to help you create a successful one-year plan that will take you to the next level.

1. Define Your Goals

Identify Key Areas: Start by identifying the key areas of your life where you want to set goals. These might include:

Personal development (e.g., learning a new skill)

Career and education (e.g., getting a promotion or completing a course)

Financial goals (e.g., saving for a vacation or paying off debt)

Health and wellness (e.g., exercising regularly or improving your diet)

Relationships and social goals (e.g., spending more time with family)

Set SMART Goals: Ensure your goals are Specific, Measurable, Achievable, Relevant, and Time-bound. For example, instead of saying "I want to save money," set a SMART goal like "I want to save $5,000 by the end of the year."

2. Break Down Your Goals

Divide Into Milestones: Break your one-year goal into smaller, manageable milestones. For example, if you want to save $5,000 by the end of the year, you can set a monthly savings goal of approximately $417.

Set Deadlines: Assign a specific deadline to each milestone. Breaking your goals into quarterly or monthly achievements makes them easier to track and gives you a clearer roadmap.

3. Create an Action Plan

List Actionable Steps: For each goal, write down the steps you need to take to achieve it. Be as specific as possible. For example, if your goal is to improve your fitness, actionable steps might include:

Sign up for a gym membership by January 15th.

Attend the gym 3 times a week.

Follow a specific workout plan starting February 1st.

Prioritize Tasks: Identify which actions are the most critical and should be prioritized. This helps you focus on what will have the greatest impact.

4. Allocate Resources

Identify Resources Needed: Consider what resources you need to achieve your goals. This might include time, money, skills, or support from others.

Budget Your Time and Finances: Allocate time in your weekly or monthly schedule to work toward your goals. If financial resources are needed, plan a budget to ensure you have enough saved or allocated for this purpose.

5. Track Your Progress

Create a Tracking System: Develop a system to track your progress throughout the year. You can use a journal, planner, or digital tools such as apps or spreadsheets.

Regular Check-Ins: Schedule monthly or quarterly reviews to assess your progress. Adjust your plan if needed, based on what's working and what isn't.

6. Stay Flexible

Adapt to Changes: Be prepared for unexpected changes or challenges. If a goal becomes less relevant or your priorities shift, it's okay to modify your plan. Flexibility is key to staying motivated and making meaningful progress.

Revisit Your Goals: At the end of each review period, revisit your original goals and milestones. Celebrate your achievements and adjust any goals that may need realignment.

7. Stay Motivated

Visualize Your Success: Keep your goals visible. Use vision boards, reminders, or affirmations to keep your focus and motivation high.

Reward Yourself: Celebrate small wins along the way. Recognizing progress, even small steps, keeps you motivated for the long term.

8. Accountability

Involve Others: Share your goals with a mentor, friend, or accountability partner who can check in on your progress and offer encouragement.

Join Groups or Communities: Engage in groups or online communities that align with your goals. This can provide support, inspiration, and networking opportunities.

9. Focus on Balance

Avoid Overcommitting: While it's great to have ambitious goals, ensure you maintain balance. Overcommitting can lead to burnout. Prioritize self-care and time for relaxation.

Create a Balanced Plan: Incorporate different aspects of your life (e.g., career, health, relationships) into your plan, so you're growing holistically and not neglecting key areas.

10. Evaluate at Year's End

End-of-Year Reflection: At the end of the year, reflect on your achievements, challenges, and growth. Evaluate what worked, what didn't, and how you can improve your planning process for the future.

Quiz

1. What specific financial goals did Abigale set in her one-year plan, and how did breaking them into smaller steps help her stay on track?

   ____

   ____

2. How did Abigale adjust her spending habits and budget to prioritize saving for an emergency fund, paying off debt, and contributing to her retirement?

   ____

   ____

3. What methods did Abigale use to stay accountable and motivated throughout the year to ensure she achieved her financial goals?

   ____

   ____

How to create a Three-year plan

Now that you have a little more time, creating a three-year plan helps you focus on long-term goals while breaking them down into achievable steps. It provides a roadmap for personal and professional development, ensuring you stay on track to achieve your objectives. Here's a step-by-step guide on how to create an effective three-year plan for your unique vision.

1. Define Your Long-Term Vision

Clarify Your Vision: Start by identifying where you want to be in three years. This could be related to various areas of your life, such as:

Career: Advancing in your current position, changing careers, or starting a business.

Personal Development: Gaining new skills, pursuing a passion, or improving work-life balance.

Financial: Building savings, reducing debt, or investing.

Health and Wellness: Achieving fitness goals, improving mental health, or adopting a healthier lifestyle.

Relationships: Building stronger relationships with family and friends, or starting a family.

Create a Vision Statement: Write a clear, motivating statement about where you see yourself in three years. This will serve as your guiding star for the plan.

2. Set SMART Goals

Specific: Be clear about what exactly you want to achieve (e.g., "Get promoted to senior manager" rather than "Improve my career").

Measurable: Define how you will measure progress (e.g., "Save $20,000 for a down payment on a house").

Achievable: Ensure your goals are realistic given your resources and time frame.

Relevant: Make sure the goals align with your values and long-term vision.

Time-bound: Include deadlines for each goal, knowing that you have a three-year time frame.

3. Break Down Your Goals Into Annual Milestones

Year 1 Milestones: Start with smaller, foundational goals that will set you up for long-term success. For example, if your three-year goal is to save $20,000, your first-year milestone could be to save $5,000.

Year 2 Milestones: Build on the progress from year one by setting intermediate goals. For example, save another $7,000 or take on more responsibility at work.

Year 3 Milestones: By this year, you should be approaching your final goal. In the savings example, this would mean reaching your $20,000 target. Ensure that year three goals focus on completing or nearing the long-term objective.

4. Create Action Steps for Each Year

For each annual milestone, break it down into smaller, actionable steps. These should be concrete actions you can take to move closer to your goal. For example:

Year 1 Action Steps:

Set up a monthly savings plan.

Identify areas to reduce spending.

Open a separate savings account for your down payment fund.

Year 2 Action Steps:

Look for additional income opportunities like freelancing or a side job.

Review and adjust your budget for increased savings.

Year 3 Action Steps:

Finalize plans for the house purchase.

Meet with a financial advisor to ensure you're on track.

5. Allocate Resources

Time: Schedule time to work on your goals, whether it's daily, weekly, or monthly. For example, set aside specific times for studying, exercising, or working on personal projects.

Money: Determine the financial resources needed for each goal and set aside a budget for it. If your goal requires investments (e.g., education, homeownership, business startup), start planning your finances early.

Skills and Support: Identify any skills you need to acquire and resources that can help you. For example, you may need to take a course, attend seminars, or seek mentorship.

6. Create a Timeline

Monthly and Quarterly Checkpoints: Break your goals into shorter intervals, such as monthly or quarterly tasks, to ensure steady progress. Review and adjust your plan regularly to keep it aligned with your changing circumstances or priorities.

Track Your Progress: Use tools like spreadsheets, journals, or apps to monitor your progress. Tracking ensures accountability and helps you stay motivated.

7. Stay Flexible and Adapt to Change

Adjust When Necessary: Life circumstances may change, so be flexible. If a goal becomes unattainable or irrelevant, reassess your priorities and adjust your plan accordingly. Stay open to new opportunities or challenges that may shift your direction.

Revisit Annually: At the end of each year, review your accomplishments and set new milestones for the upcoming year. Celebrate your successes and learn from any setbacks. Make adjustments to your plan as needed.

8. Motivation and Accountability

Visualize Success: Keep a vision board or list of your long-term goals where you can see them daily. This will remind you of what you're working towards and keep you motivated.

Reward Milestones: As you reach your milestones, reward yourself to stay motivated. Small rewards can help maintain focus and encourage consistent progress.

Accountability Partner: Share your goals with a mentor, friend, or family member. Regular check-ins with someone who holds you accountable can help you stay on track.

9. Evaluate Risks and Challenges

Identify Potential Challenges: Consider any obstacles you may face over the next three years, such as job changes, health issues, or unexpected expenses. Anticipate these challenges so you can develop contingency plans.

Develop Solutions: For each potential challenge, create a backup plan. For example, if you're saving money and a job loss occurs, adjust your budget to prioritize essential expenses and find ways to earn supplemental income.

10. Reflect and Adjust

Regular Self-Evaluation: Throughout the three years, reflect on your progress and adjust your goals and milestones if necessary. Life changes, and your goals may need to evolve along with it.

How to create a Five-year plan

The ultimate plan is creating a five-year plan that helps you set a long-term vision for your personal and professional goals, allowing you to strategize and work toward meaningful achievements. Here's a comprehensive guide to crafting a successful five-year plan that you will be proud of.

1. Establish Your Vision

Envision Your Future: Start by imagining where you want to be in five years. Think about various aspects of your life:

Career: Where do you see yourself professionally? Do you want a promotion, a career change, or to start your own business?

Personal Development: What skills do you want to acquire? Do you want to further your education, learn a new language, or improve certain talents?

Financial Goals: Do you want to save for a home, invest in stocks, or build a retirement fund?

Health and Wellness: What are your long-term health and fitness goals?

Relationships and Social Life: Where do you want to be in your relationships with family, friends, or a partner?

Create a Vision Statement: Write a statement describing your ideal life in five years. This will serve as a guiding star for your plan.

2. Set Specific, Measurable Goals

SMART Goals: Break your vision into SMART goals—goals that are Specific, Measurable, Achievable, Relevant, and Time-bound. For example:

Career Goal: "Become a department manager at my company by the end of year three."

Financial Goal: "Save $50,000 for a house down payment in five years."

Personal Development Goal: "Complete an MBA program within four years."

Health Goal: "Lose 20 pounds and run a half marathon by the end of year two."

Prioritize: Rank your goals in terms of importance and feasibility, so you know where to focus your energy first.

3. Break Down Goals into Annual Milestones

Year 1 Milestones: Start with foundational actions that set you on the right path. For example, if your goal is to save $50,000 in five years, your first-year milestone could be saving $10,000.

Year 2 Milestones: Build on your progress from year one. This might include furthering your education, expanding your professional network, or increasing your savings.

Year 3-5 Milestones: By years three to five, you should be making significant headway toward your long-term goals, such as advancing in your career, achieving major financial objectives, or completing educational programs.

4. Create Actionable Steps for Each Year

For each milestone, break it down into smaller, actionable steps. These are concrete tasks you can work on regularly to reach your milestones. For example:

Career Steps:

In year 1, attend relevant training programs and network with key professionals.

In year 2, apply for leadership positions or take on more responsibilities at work.

Financial Steps:

In year 1, set a monthly budget to save $1,000 per month.

In year 3, explore investment opportunities to grow your savings.

5. Allocate Resources

Time: Plan your time wisely by scheduling regular intervals to work on your goals. For example, set aside specific times each week to study, work out, or focus on a side project.

Financial Resources: Estimate the financial resources needed for each goal (e.g., education costs, travel, or investments). Create a budget that allocates funds to your long-term goals.

Skills and Knowledge: Identify what skills or knowledge you need to achieve your goals, and find ways to acquire them, such as enrolling in courses, finding mentors, or reading relevant materials.

6. Track Your Progress

Create a Tracking System: Develop a system to track your progress on a monthly, quarterly, or yearly basis. You can use digital tools like spreadsheets or apps, or simply keep a detailed journal.

Regular Check-ins: Schedule regular check-ins (e.g., every quarter) to evaluate your progress. Adjust your actions or goals if necessary to stay on track or accommodate changing circumstances.

7. Anticipate Challenges and Develop Contingency Plans

Identify Potential Obstacles: Consider challenges you might face over the five years, such as job changes, health issues, or family commitments. Being proactive can help you navigate them more effectively.

Create Backup Plans: Develop contingency plans for each key area. For example, if saving $50,000 becomes difficult due to a job loss, adjust your budget or explore alternative income streams.

8. Stay Flexible and Adapt

Be Open to Change: Life can be unpredictable, so remain flexible. If priorities shift or new opportunities arise, don't hesitate to revise your goals and plans. Staying adaptable ensures that your plan remains realistic and relevant.

Evaluate Annually: At the end of each year, review your progress and adjust your milestones and action steps for the following years. Celebrate successes and learn from any setbacks.

9. Motivation and Accountability

Visualize Your Success: Keep your goals visible through vision boards, daily affirmations, or written reminders. This will help you stay focused and motivated over the long term.

Reward Yourself: Celebrate reaching key milestones, no matter how small. Rewards help maintain momentum and make the journey enjoyable.

Accountability Partner: Share your goals with a mentor, friend, or family member. Regularly updating someone on your progress can keep you accountable and motivated.

10. Create Balance in Your Plan

Avoid Overloading: Don't try to achieve everything at once. Balance your goals across different areas of life (e.g., career, personal, financial, health) and give yourself realistic timelines to avoid burnout.

Ensure Self-Care: Make sure your plan includes time for rest, relaxation, and personal well-being. Success is best enjoyed when it doesn't come at the expense of your physical or mental health.

11. Long-Term Reflection

At the Five-Year Mark: When you reach the end of your five-year plan, reflect on what you've accomplished. Celebrate your achievements, acknowledge areas where you grew, and take stock of what you've learned.

Plan for the Next Phase: Use your progress to set new long-term goals for the next five years or beyond, building on your accomplishments and aiming for even greater success.

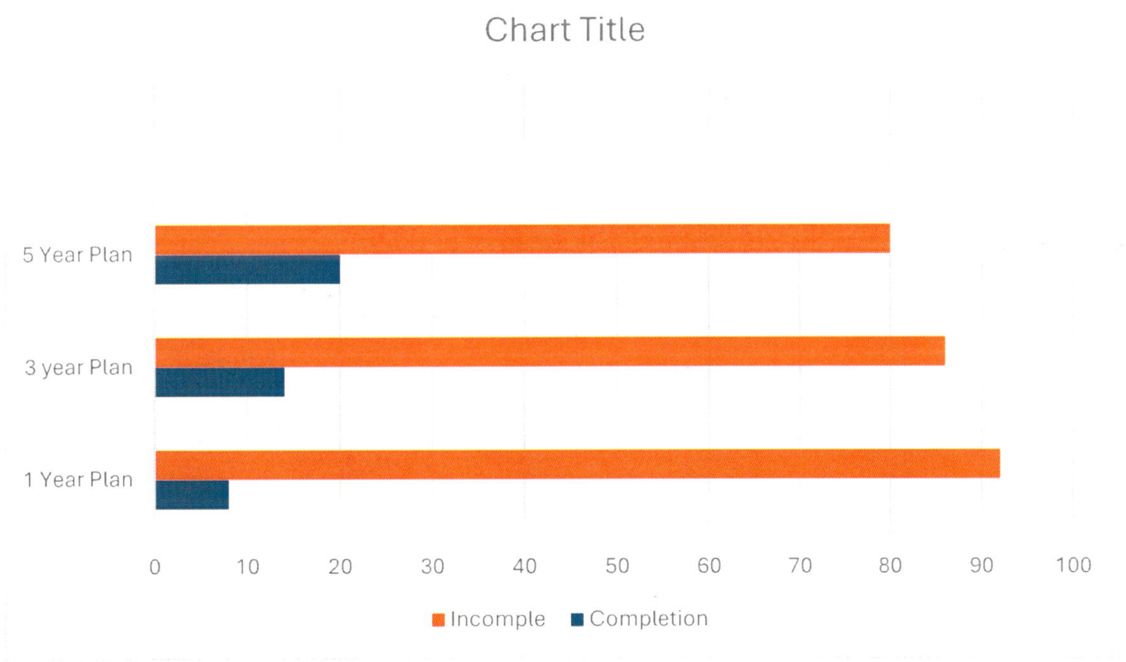

The Snowball Method

Elizabeth was looking forward to retirement after her 59th birthday, but her excitement was dampened by the weight of her debts. Over the years, she had accumulated credit card balances, a car loan, and other obligations that seemed insurmountable. With a fixed income on the horizon, she knew she needed a plan to regain financial freedom.

One day, while listening to a financial professional webinar, Elizabeth learned about the snowball method for debt repayment. This strategy involves paying off debts from the smallest balance to the largest, regardless of interest rates, to build momentum and motivation.

Implementing the Snowball Method

Elizabeth took the following steps to tackle her debts:

List All Debts: She compiled a list of her debts, excluding her mortgage, ordered from the smallest to the largest balance

Make Minimum Payments: She ensured all debts received their minimum payments to avoid penalties

Focus on the Smallest Debt: Elizabeth directed any extra funds toward the smallest debt, aiming to pay it off first

Roll Over Payments: Once the smallest debt was cleared, she applied the amount she had been paying on it to the next smallest debt, in addition to its minimum payment

Repeat the Process: She continued this pattern, progressively eliminating each debt

The Transformation

Within a year, Elizabeth witnessed significant progress. By systematically paying off her smaller debts, she freed up additional funds to tackle larger ones. This approach not only reduced her overall debt but also boosted her confidence and financial literacy.

As she approached retirement, Elizabeth felt a renewed sense of security. The snowball method had provided a clear path to debt freedom, allowing her to look forward to her golden years without the looming burden of debt.

Reflection

Elizabeth's journey underscores the effectiveness of the snowball method in managing and eliminating debt. By focusing on one debt at a time, she was able to make consistent progress and achieve financial stability before retirement.

The snowball method is a debt reduction strategy that focuses on paying off your debts from the smallest balance to the largest, regardless of interest rates. This method helps build momentum and motivation as you achieve small victories by eliminating smaller debts first. Here's a step-by-step guide on how to use the snowball method to get out of debt.

1. List All Your Debts

Write Down Every Debt: Start by making a comprehensive list of all your debts, including credit cards, student loans, car loans, medical bills, and personal loans.

Organize by Balance Size: Arrange your debts in order from the smallest balance to the largest, regardless of the interest rates.

Example:

Debt A: $500 (credit card)

Debt B: $1,500 (medical bill)

Debt C: $3,000 (student loan)

Debt D: $8,000 (car loan)

2. Make Minimum Payments on All Debts

Pay the Minimum on Every Debt: While focusing on paying off the smallest debt first, ensure you continue to make at least the minimum payments on all other debts to avoid late fees and penalties.

3. Attack the Smallest Debt First

Put Extra Money Toward the Smallest Debt: Take any extra money you can find (from your budget, side jobs, or cutting expenses) and apply it toward the smallest debt.

Example: If your minimum payment for Debt A is $25, but you can add an extra $100, pay $125 toward that debt each month until it's completely paid off.

4. Celebrate Small Wins

Pay Off the Smallest Debt: Once the smallest debt is fully paid off, celebrate the achievement! This is a motivational boost that keeps you excited about the debt payoff process.

Roll Over the Payment: Take the total amount you were paying on the now-eliminated debt (both the minimum payment and any extra payments) and add it to the minimum payment for the next smallest debt.

5. Repeat the Process for the Next Debt

Move to the Next Smallest Debt: Now that Debt A is paid off, focus on Debt B. Take the amount you were paying toward Debt A and add it to your minimum payment for Debt B.

Example: If the minimum payment for Debt B was $50, and you were paying $125 on Debt A, you now pay $175 toward Debt B each month.

Continue to pay the minimums on all other debts.

6. Continue Building Momentum

Keep Rolling Payments: As each debt is paid off, roll the total amount you were paying toward the previous debt to the next one. This creates a snowball effect where your payments grow larger as you tackle bigger debts.

Example:

You finish paying Debt B. Now, you take the $175 you were paying on Debt B and add it to the minimum payment for Debt C.

If Debt C's minimum payment is $100, you now pay $275 toward Debt C each month.

7. Watch the Snowball Grow

Larger Payments on Bigger Debts: As your snowball grows, you'll be paying larger and larger amounts toward your remaining debts, making it easier to tackle even larger balances.

Example: Once Debt C is paid off, roll that $275 toward Debt D. If Debt D's minimum payment is $150, you now pay $425 toward Debt D each month.

8. Stay Consistent

Stick to the Plan: The key to the snowball method is consistency. Even if it feels slow at the beginning, the momentum you gain as you eliminate debts will build, and you'll start seeing significant progress.

Avoid New Debt: While using the snowball method, it's important not to take on any new debt, which could derail your progress. Focus on living within your means and avoiding unnecessary expenses.

9. Celebrate Becoming Debt-Free

Enjoy Your Progress: Once all your debts are paid off, take time to celebrate your financial freedom. You've achieved something incredible by using discipline and persistence.

Plan for the Future: Now that you're debt-free, use the money that was going toward debt payments to build savings, invest, and reach other financial goals.

Why the Snowball Method Works

Psychological Wins: By paying off smaller debts quickly, you gain a sense of accomplishment, which boosts motivation to continue.

Focus on Simplicity: Instead of worrying about interest rates and trying to calculate the best financial return, the snowball method is simple and easy to follow, focusing on progress and results.

Momentum: As each debt is eliminated, the amount you can apply to the next debt increases, creating a snowball effect that accelerates debt repayment.

Quiz

1. How did Elizabeth prioritize her debts using the snowball method, and what impact did focusing on smaller debts first have on her motivation?

   ____

   ____

2. What steps did Elizabeth take to ensure she maintained consistent payments on all her debts while aggressively paying down her smallest balance?

   ____

   ____

3. How did eliminating her debts with the snowball method change Elizabeth's financial outlook and sense of security as she prepared for retirement?

   ____

   ____

The Avalanche Method

Joseph found himself overwhelmed by debt. Between credit card balances, student loans, and a car payment, his financial situation seemed bleak. What made it worse was the high interest on some of his debts, which was causing them to grow faster than he could manage. With retirement still a couple of decades away, Joseph knew he needed to take control of his finances now, or his future would be at risk.

One day, after researching debt repayment strategies, Joseph learned about the Avalanche Method. Unlike the snowball method, which focuses on paying off the smallest debts first, the avalanche method targets the debt with the highest interest rate. This approach made sense to Joseph—he knew that if he tackled his most expensive debts first, he'd save money on interest in the long run.

Implementing the Avalanche Method

Joseph took the following steps to regain control of his finances:

List All Debts: He created a list of all his debts, noting the interest rates and minimum payments for each.

Prioritize the Highest-Interest Debt: The credit card debt with a 20% interest rate topped the list, followed by his personal loan with a 12% rate.

Make Minimum Payments on All Debts: Joseph made sure to pay the minimum required amount on all his debts to avoid penalties.

Apply Extra Payments to the Highest-Interest Debt: Any additional money Joseph could save each month—by cutting back on unnecessary spending—went straight toward the credit card debt.

Repeat the Process: Once his highest-interest debt was paid off, Joseph redirected the funds he had been using for that payment to the next highest-interest debt, and so on.

The Turning Point

In the first few months, it felt slow. Joseph wasn't seeing immediate results like the snowball method might have offered, but he reminded himself of the bigger picture—saving thousands on interest in the long run. After about a year, he paid off his high-interest credit card completely. This gave him momentum to tackle his personal loan next, and then his car loan.

Each time Joseph eliminated a debt, more of his income became available to pay off the next one. His financial situation started to shift dramatically. He no longer felt buried under bills, and instead, he felt in control of his money. With each debt he eliminated, he saved hundreds, if not thousands, of dollars in interest.

The Long-Term Impact

By the time Joseph turned 45, he was completely debt-free. His decision to use the avalanche method not only saved him money in the short term but also set him up for a stronger financial future. Without debt holding him back, Joseph began to focus on building his retirement savings. He started maxing out his 401(k) contributions and made smart investments that further grew his wealth.

As Joseph approached his retirement years, he reflected on how the avalanche method had changed his financial life. By eliminating high-interest debt, he had set the stage for a secure and comfortable retirement, free from financial stress. What had once seemed like an overwhelming burden had become a turning point in his journey toward financial freedom.

Joseph's life before retirement was now defined by smart money management, all thanks to a method that had prioritized tackling his most costly debts first.

The avalanche method is a debt repayment strategy that focuses on paying off debts with the highest interest rates first, which can save you more money on interest over time. While it may take longer to pay off your first debt compared to the snowball method, this approach minimizes the total interest paid, helping you get out of debt faster overall. Here's a step-by-step guide on how to use the avalanche method to get out of debt.

1. List All Your Debts

Write Down Every Debt: Create a detailed list of all your debts, including the outstanding balance, minimum monthly payment, and interest rates for each.

Organize by Interest Rate: Rank your debts from highest interest rate to lowest, regardless of the balance amount.

Example:

Debt A: $1,000 balance, 20% interest (credit card)

Debt B: $5,000 balance, 15% interest (personal loan)

Debt C: $3,000 balance, 10% interest (student loan)

Debt D: $8,000 balance, 5% interest (car loan)

2. Make Minimum Payments on All Debts

Stay Current on All Accounts: Make the minimum payment on each debt every month to avoid late fees and damage to your credit score.

This ensures that while you're focusing on the highest-interest debt, the others remain in good standing.

3. Put Extra Money Toward the Highest-Interest Debt

Focus on the Highest-Interest Debt First: Once you've made minimum payments on all your debts, direct any extra money you have toward the debt with the highest interest rate (in this case, Debt A with 20% interest).

Example: If your minimum payment for Debt A is $50, and you have an extra $100 to put toward debt, pay $150 toward Debt A each month until it's paid off.

4. Pay Off the First Debt

Eliminate the Highest-Interest Debt: Continue making larger payments toward the highest-interest debt until it is fully paid off. Since this debt has the highest interest rate, paying it off first reduces the total interest you'll pay over time.

Once this debt is cleared, you'll free up the money you were using to pay it off.

5. Move to the Next Highest-Interest Debt

Focus on the Next Debt: Once Debt A is paid off, take the total amount you were paying on it and apply it to the next highest-interest debt (Debt B with 15% interest).

Example: If your minimum payment for Debt B is $100, and you were paying $150 on Debt A, now pay $250 toward Debt B each month.

Continue making minimum payments on all lower-interest debts.

6. Repeat the Process

Avalanche the Payments: As each high-interest debt is paid off, continue rolling the payments into the next highest-interest debt.

This creates an "avalanche effect," where the amount you're able to pay on each subsequent debt grows larger, allowing you to pay off each remaining debt more quickly.

Example:

After Debt B is paid off, take the $250 and add it to the minimum payment for Debt C (10% interest).

If Debt C's minimum payment is $75, you'll now pay $325 toward Debt C each month.

7. Keep Momentum

Stick to the Plan: The avalanche method can feel slow at first since you are tackling the highest-interest debt, which may also have a larger balance. However, stick with it because the payoff in reduced interest will help you get out of debt faster in the long run.

Avoid New Debt: To stay on track, avoid taking on any new debt, especially high-interest debt like credit cards. Focus on living within your means and maintaining a disciplined budget.

8. Celebrate Becoming Debt-Free

Pay Off All Debts: Once you've worked through all your debts, you'll not only be debt-free but will have saved a significant amount in interest compared to other methods.

Celebrate and Reinvest: Celebrate this achievement, and then consider redirecting the money you were using for debt payments into savings, investments, or other financial goals, such as building an emergency fund.

Why the Avalanche Method Works

Reduces Interest Costs: By focusing on high-interest debt first, you minimize the amount of interest you pay over time. This makes the avalanche method the most cost-efficient strategy for getting out of debt.

Faster Payoff for Large Debts: The avalanche method helps you tackle large, high-interest debts early, preventing interest from piling up and allowing you to get ahead of your debts.

Financial Logic: The avalanche method is based on mathematics, aiming to reduce your overall debt burden in the most financially efficient way, even if it doesn't provide the immediate psychological wins of the snowball method.

Pros and Cons of the Avalanche Method

Pros

Saves Money on Interest: The biggest advantage is that you'll pay less interest overall, which can save you hundreds or even thousands of dollars over time.

Gets You Out of Debt Faster: By reducing the total amount you owe on interest, you can become debt-free more quickly.

Best for High-Interest Debt: This method is ideal for those with significant high-interest debt, such as credit cards or payday loans.

Cons

Takes Longer to See Progress: If your highest-interest debt also has a large balance, it may take a while to fully pay it off. This can be discouraging for some people who prefer more immediate results.

Less Motivating: Unlike the snowball method, the avalanche method doesn't give you quick wins. It requires discipline and patience to see the long-term benefit.

How to Stay Motivated with the Avalanche Method

Track Your Progress: Keep a visual record of how much you're saving on interest by using the avalanche method. Seeing those savings grow can keep you motivated.

Focus on the Long-Term Goal: Remember that the avalanche method is the most financially efficient way to get out of debt. Even though it may feel slow, every payment gets you closer to being debt-free while saving money.

Celebrate Milestones: Set small milestones for yourself along the way, such as paying off 25%, 50%, or 75% of your total debt. Reward yourself when you reach each one to stay motivated.

<u>Quiz</u>

1. How did Joseph decide which debts to prioritize using the avalanche method, and what impact did paying off high-interest debts first have on his long-term financial savings?

   ____

   ____

2. What changes did Joseph make to his spending habits to free up extra funds for paying down his highest-interest debts?

   ____

   ____

3. How did eliminating high-interest debt through the avalanche method help Joseph build a stronger foundation for retirement savings and long-term financial security?

   ____

   ____

List of Assets

Rachel found herself at a crossroads. She had a stable job in marketing, but she realized that her current savings wouldn't be enough to ensure a comfortable retirement. She had always lived within her means, but between daily expenses and her children's education costs, she hadn't built up significant savings. One evening, while discussing retirement with a close friend, she was struck by the realization that her paycheck wouldn't be her only source of income if she invested wisely.

Determined to change her financial future, Rachel decided to start learning about investing in assets. She didn't know much at first at the age of 43, but after reading books, attending workshops, and watching online tutorials, she gained a clearer understanding of how to grow her wealth. The idea that investing could provide passive income excited her, especially with retirement not too far off.

Rachel's Investment Journey

Step 1: Real Estate Investment Her first major investment was in real estate. Rachel bought a small rental property in a growing neighborhood with a modest mortgage. After renovating it, she rented it out, which provided her with a steady monthly income stream. She used this rental income to pay down the mortgage faster, and within a few years, the property was generating pure profit.

Step 2: Dividend-Paying Stocks Rachel also began investing in dividend-paying stocks. She researched companies with a strong track record of paying dividends and started purchasing shares over time. Every quarter, she received dividends, which she reinvested to grow her portfolio further. As her stock portfolio increased, so did her passive income.

Step 3: A Small Business Investment Later, Rachel invested in a local small business—a cafe run by a friend. She became a silent partner, contributing capital in exchange for a share of the profits. The business thrived, and Rachel's investment began providing a solid supplemental income stream.

How It Changed Rachel's Financial Future

Within a decade, Rachel's smart investments had dramatically altered her financial direction. By the time she was nearing retirement, she had multiple streams of income:

Her rental property was fully paid off, and the rent provided a reliable monthly cash flow.

Her dividend stocks had grown into a sizable portfolio, offering her quarterly payments without having to lift a finger.

The cafe continued to generate passive income, even as Rachel considered stepping away from her full-time career.

Now in her mid-50s, Rachel felt a sense of financial security she hadn't thought possible. Instead of relying solely on her job and savings, her investments had turned into a steady stream of supplemental income. She no longer worried about whether she could retire comfortably or how she would handle unexpected expenses.

A New Chapter Before Retirement

Thanks to her investments, Rachel was able to reduce her work hours and focus on the things she loved. She traveled more, spent time with her family, and even began mentoring younger women on financial independence and investing. Her decision to invest in assets had not only changed her financial situation but had given her the freedom to live life on her terms.

As Rachel prepared for retirement, she knew she had built a solid foundation that would continue to support her well into her golden years. Her assets had become more than just financial tools—they had become the key to her long-term security and happiness.

Here's a list of profitable assets that can generate income or appreciate in value over time, depending on your financial goals and risk tolerance.

1. Stocks

Growth Stocks: Companies with potential for significant earnings growth.

Dividend-Paying Stocks: Companies that regularly pay dividends, providing passive income.

Index Funds & ETFs: Low-cost, diversified funds that track market indices like the S&P 500.

2. Real Estate

Rental Properties: Residential or commercial properties that generate rental income.

Real Estate Investment Trusts (REITs): Investments in real estate without owning physical property, offering dividends from rental income.

Fix-and-Flip Properties: Buying undervalued properties, renovating, and selling for a profit.

3. Bonds

Government Bonds: Low-risk bonds issued by the government, offering fixed interest payments.

Corporate Bonds: Bonds issued by corporations, usually with higher returns than government bonds but higher risk.

Municipal Bonds: Bonds issued by local governments, often with tax advantages.

4. Commodities

Precious Metals: Gold, silver, and platinum, which can serve as a hedge against inflation.

Oil and Natural Gas: Investing in energy commodities or related ETFs.

5. Cryptocurrency

Bitcoin and Altcoins: Digital currencies that can appreciate in value, though they carry high volatility.

Stablecoins: Cryptocurrencies pegged to a stable asset, offering lower risk and sometimes yield opportunities.

6. Peer-to-Peer Lending

Lending Platforms: Providing loans to individuals or small businesses through platforms like LendingClub or Prosper, which offer interest income.

7. Business Ownership

Start a Business: Creating and running your own company can generate income and equity.

Invest in a Franchise: Buying into a proven business model with ongoing support.

8. Collectibles

Art, Antiques, and Memorabilia: Items that appreciate over time, especially if they are rare or in high demand.

Luxury Goods: Watches, jewelry, or designer items that retain or increase their value.

9. Intellectual Property

Royalties from Books, Music, or Patents: Creating content or owning rights to intellectual property can generate ongoing passive income.

10. Farmland and Timberland

Agricultural Land: Buying land that can be used for farming, which provides rental income and potential appreciation.

Timberland: Land with trees that can be harvested for wood, offering long-term growth and income.

11. Precious Metals IRAs

Self-Directed IRAs: Investing in precious metals through an Individual Retirement Account for tax benefits and portfolio diversification.

12. Private Equity or Venture Capital

Startup Investments: Funding early-stage businesses with high growth potential, though the risks are higher.

Private Equity Funds: Investing in private companies or taking over undervalued public companies to restructure and sell for a profit.

13. Foreign Currencies (Forex)

Currency Trading: Buying and selling foreign currencies to profit from exchange rate fluctuations, though this carries significant risk.

14. Luxury Real Estate

High-End Properties: Investing in luxury properties that appreciate due to their exclusivity and location.

15. Agriculture and Livestock

Farming Operations: Owning and operating farms or livestock, which can provide income through crop sales or animal husbandry.

16. Farmland Crowdfunding

Platforms like FarmTogether: Investing in fractional shares of farmland to earn rental income and appreciation.

17. Renewable Energy Investments

Solar or Wind Projects: Investing in green energy infrastructure can provide returns through government incentives and rising energy demand.

18. Water Rights

Water Resources: Buying water rights or infrastructure can be a valuable asset, especially in areas with growing water scarcity.

Quiz

1. How did Rachel diversify her investments across different asset classes like real estate, dividend-paying stocks, and small business ventures, and how did this diversification contribute to her financial security before retirement?

   ____

   ____

2. What steps did Rachel take to educate herself about investing, and how can someone replicate her approach to making informed financial decisions about assets?

   ____

   ____

3. How did Rachel's investment strategy help her create multiple streams of passive income, and how can others use a similar strategy to supplement their income as they prepare for retirement?

   ____

   ____

Earn Income

Ducati had just finished high school and wasn't sure what his future held. College didn't feel like the right path for him, and he didn't want to get stuck in a 9-to-5 job he didn't love. Growing up, he had watched his father run a small barbershop in their neighborhood, cutting hair for the same loyal customers for years. As a kid, Ducati would spend weekends at the shop, sweeping floors, chatting with customers, and watching his father skillfully handle the clippers.

One day, his father handed him the clippers and said, "Why don't you give it a try?" With some guidance, Ducati gave his first haircut, and it was surprisingly good. The feeling of shaping someone's look, and the satisfaction of seeing a happy customer, sparked something in him.

Ducati decided to take barbering seriously. His father taught him everything he knew—how to cut different styles, how to manage a client base, and how to run a barbershop. By the time he was 23, Ducati was skilled enough to handle clients on his own. Rather than working for someone else, he chose the path of self-employment, determined to follow in his father's footsteps.

Building His Own Business

Step 1: Starting Small Ducati started by cutting hair from his father's shop, slowly building his own client list. He offered affordable prices to attract new clients and spread the word through social media. His reputation for clean fades, detailed lineups, and a friendly atmosphere began to grow.

Step 2: Building Relationships Barbering wasn't just about haircuts; it was about relationships. Ducati learned from his father that people come to barbers not just for a service but for the connection. He remembered names, asked about their families, and made every customer feel valued. Word of mouth spread quickly in their community, and soon, he had a steady stream of clients who trusted him.

Step 3: Expanding His Skills Ducati didn't stop at just the basics. He continued learning new techniques, from modern styles to beard grooming, and even started offering premium services like hot towel shaves and hair care consultations. This helped him stand out and charge more for his services.

Step 4: Opening His Own Shop After a few years, with the support of his father and the savings he had built, Ducati opened his own barbershop. He called it "Ducati's Cuts," a nod to the skills his father had passed down to him. The shop became a place where people felt at home—an essential part of the community.

The Long-Term Payoff

By the time Ducati hit his 30s, his barbershop was thriving. He had hired two additional barbers, and the business was running smoothly. The decision to become self-employed at 23 was paying off in ways he hadn't expected. Not only was he earning a steady income, but he also had the freedom to set his own hours, choose his clients, and control the direction of his business.

Because he was self-employed, Ducati had learned to manage his finances carefully. He put money aside for taxes, invested in high-quality equipment, and even started saving for retirement early on. His shop became a neighborhood fixture, known for both quality haircuts and the warm atmosphere he fostered.

Looking to the Future

Ducati realized that barbering had given him something far greater than just an income. It had given him independence, the ability to build wealth, and the satisfaction of running his own business. He planned to expand his shop further, maybe even open a second location.

Most importantly, Ducati had learned that the skills his father had taught him weren't just about cutting hair—they were about building a life of financial stability and freedom. At a young age, he had made the choice to be self-employed, and now, as he looked ahead to his future, he knew he had laid the foundation for long-term success.

In the long run, being self-employed had given him not just an income but a sense of pride, fulfillment, and a path to a secure financial future.

A successful way to earn income involves combining active and passive income streams, leveraging skills, and using time efficiently. Below is a detailed approach to earning a sustainable income:

1. Develop Marketable Skills

Identify High-Demand Skills: Start by learning or refining a skill that is in demand in your field, such as digital marketing, software development, graphic design, or data analysis. These skills are valuable across industries and offer high earning potential.

Invest in Education: Take online courses, attend workshops, or earn certifications to improve your expertise and credibility.

Freelance or Consulting: Use platforms like Upwork, Fiverr, or LinkedIn to offer your skills to clients. Freelancing or consulting allows you to set your rates and control your schedule.

2. Start a Side Business

Service-Based Business: A service-based business can provide steady cash flow. Examples include tutoring, personal training, web design, or social media management. Services often have low start-up costs and high profitability.

Product-Based Business: If you have a product idea, consider selling it on platforms like Etsy, Amazon, or through your own e-commerce website. Look for products with low production costs but high demand to ensure profitability.

Drop shipping: With minimal inventory, drop shipping allows you to sell products through an online store while a third party handles fulfillment. This reduces overhead costs and risk.

3. Create Passive Income Streams

Investing in Dividend Stocks: By purchasing shares of companies that pay regular dividends, you can earn income without active involvement. Dividend reinvestment can compound returns over time.

Real Estate Rentals: If you have capital to invest, purchasing a rental property can generate monthly cash flow. Platforms like Airbnb also allow you to rent out properties short-term for potentially higher returns.

Peer-to-Peer Lending: Platforms like Prosper or LendingClub allow you to lend money to individuals or businesses for a return on investment. This creates a passive income stream with moderate risk.

Create Digital Products: Develop e-books, online courses, or stock photos that can be sold repeatedly with minimal upkeep. Once the product is created, you can generate income passively through sales.

4. Leverage Technology and Automation

Use Automation Tools: Automate parts of your business, such as marketing, customer service, or inventory management, using tools like HubSpot, Mailchimp, or Shopify. Automation frees up your time to focus on growing your business.

Digital Marketing: Use social media, SEO, and email marketing to promote your services or products, expanding your reach to more customers without requiring substantial ongoing effort.

5. Network and Collaborate

Build a Strong Network: Connect with professionals in your field to gain referrals, partnerships, and mentorship. Attending industry events and participating in online communities helps you expand your opportunities.

Collaborate with Others: Consider partnering with people who have complementary skills or businesses. This can open up new markets or reduce operational burdens.

6. Invest for the Long Term

Stocks and Bonds: A diversified investment portfolio of stocks and bonds can grow your wealth over time. You can invest through tax-advantaged accounts like a 401(k) or IRA to maximize returns.

Index Funds and ETFs: These funds are less risky and provide steady returns. They track the market or a sector, offering broad diversification and reducing the chance of losing your principal.

7. Scale Your Income

Hire Help: As your business or freelance work grows, hire employees or subcontractors to take on tasks. This allows you to focus on high-value activities that increase your income.

Licensing or Franchising: If your business model is successful, you can scale by licensing your brand or selling franchises. This allows others to use your business model while you earn a percentage of their revenue.

Reinvest in Growth: Put a portion of your earnings back into the business to expand your reach, hire better talent, or improve technology, which can accelerate your income growth.

8. Create Multiple Income Streams

Diversify: Don't rely on a single source of income. Create multiple streams by combining a job or business with side hustles, investments, and passive income sources.

Online Courses or Webinars: Once you have expertise in a subject, create courses or host webinars. Platforms like Teachable or Udemy allow you to monetize your knowledge.

Quiz

1. How did Ducati leverage the skills he learned from his father and gradually build a client base, and what lessons can be applied when starting a business with limited resources?

   ____

   ____

2. What strategies did Ducati use to grow his barbershop from offering basic services to premium options, and how can diversifying services help new entrepreneurs scale their businesses over time?

   ____

   ____

3. How did Ducati's focus on building strong relationships with clients contribute to the success of his business, and why is fostering connections important when starting and growing a business?

   ____

   ____

Borrowing

Zoey had always dreamed of running her own business. She worked a stable job in retail but longed for something more fulfilling. After years of saving a little here and there, she knew she didn't have enough to launch her business on her own. However, she had a solid plan—a vision for an online boutique that would sell handmade, eco-friendly clothing. All she needed was some capital to get started.

Borrowing Money to Start Her Business

Zoey decided to take out a small business loan. After carefully researching her options, she found a lender offering a low-interest loan designed for young entrepreneurs. Zoey borrowed $25,000, which she used to build her online store, purchase initial inventory, and invest in marketing. With a business plan in hand, she was confident this was the right decision.

Step 1: Launching the Business With the loan, Zoey hired a web designer, set up a professional website, and stocked her online boutique with the clothing she had sourced from eco-friendly suppliers. She used the remaining funds to create a marketing campaign on social media, targeting people who cared about sustainable fashion. Her business, "Zoey's Eco Threads," quickly gained traction. Customers loved the unique designs and the environmentally conscious mission behind her products.

Making Smart Investments

As her boutique began generating sales, Zoey didn't stop at just paying off her loan and covering her business expenses. She wanted her money to work for her. Zoey decided to invest a portion of her profits into the stock market, choosing companies aligned with her values—green energy and sustainable businesses.

She also invested in mutual funds, which allowed her to grow her wealth slowly but steadily. These investments helped her build a financial cushion for her business and personal life, ensuring she had funds to fall back on if sales ever slowed down.

Paying Off Personal Debts

Zoey wasn't just focused on growing her business—she wanted to take control of her personal finances too. She still had lingering student loans and credit card debt from her early twenties. After setting aside a portion of her business profits for savings and investments, Zoey used the rest to aggressively pay down her personal debts.

She started with the credit card debt, which carried the highest interest rate. Within a year, she had wiped out the balance. Next, she tackled her student loans. By living frugally, budgeting carefully, and using a portion of her growing income from the business and investments, she paid off the remainder of her loans.

The Transformation

By the time Zoey turned 32, her life looked completely different. Her online boutique was thriving, consistently bringing in profits, and her investments had grown significantly. She was debt-free, having paid off both her business loan and all her personal debts. What had once seemed like an overwhelming challenge—borrowing money, launching a business, and managing personal debt—was now a success story she could be proud of.

The Long-Term Payoff

Zoey had not only built a successful business but also secured her financial future through smart investments and responsible debt management. The combination of her business profits, investments, and newfound financial freedom allowed her to start thinking bigger—opening a physical storefront and even expanding her product line.

The decision to borrow money to launch her business, invest wisely, and take control of her personal debt had completely changed the financial direction of Zoey's life. Now, she was in control, with both her business and personal finances thriving. Zoey's story was proof that with the right plan, persistence, and smart money management, it was possible to turn a dream into a reality.

Borrowing finances can be a useful tool when done responsibly, whether to fund a business, buy a home, or manage personal expenses. Below are the best ways to borrow money, tailored to different needs and financial situations:

1. Personal Loans

Best For: Consolidating debt, major purchases, or personal expenses.

Where to Get It: Banks, credit unions, or online lenders.

Benefits:

Fixed interest rates and predictable payments.

Can be used for a variety of purposes.

No collateral required for unsecured personal loans.

Considerations: Interest rates can be higher if you have bad credit, and missing payments can damage your credit score.

2. Home Equity Loan or Line of Credit (HELOC)

Best For: Large expenses, such as home renovations, education, or debt consolidation.

Where to Get It: Banks and credit unions.

Benefits:

Lower interest rates compared to personal loans since the loan is secured by your home.

Tax-deductible interest (if the loan is used for home improvements).

With a HELOC, you can borrow only what you need and repay over time, making it flexible.

Considerations: Your home serves as collateral, so if you default on payments, you risk foreclosure.

3. Credit Cards

Best For: Short-term financing for smaller expenses or emergencies.

Where to Get It: Banks, credit unions, and online credit card providers.

Benefits:

Convenient and widely accepted.

Potential to earn rewards, cashback, or travel points.

0% interest promotional periods with balance transfers or new cards.

Considerations: High interest rates if balances are not paid off in full each month. Can lead to debt accumulation if not managed carefully.

4. Peer-to-Peer (P2P) Lending

Best For: Individuals who may not qualify for traditional loans or are looking for competitive interest rates.

Where to Get It: Online platforms like LendingClub, Prosper, or Upstart.

Benefits:

Flexible terms and often lower rates than credit cards or personal loans from traditional banks.

Faster approval process with less paperwork.

Considerations: Higher risk of rejection if you have poor credit, and fees may apply.

5. Business Loans

Best For: Starting or expanding a business, purchasing equipment, or managing cash flow.

Where to Get It: Banks, Small Business Administration (SBA), online lenders, or microfinance institutions.

Benefits:

SBA loans often have favorable terms for small businesses.

Larger loan amounts available compared to personal loans.

Can help grow your business, increase revenue, and improve credit if used wisely.

Considerations: Requires a strong business plan and good credit. Collateral may be needed for larger loans.

6. Auto Loan

Best For: Financing the purchase of a vehicle.

Where to Get It: Banks, credit unions, dealerships, and online lenders.

Benefits:

Competitive interest rates, especially for new or used vehicles.

Fixed monthly payments make it easy to budget.

Lenders often have fast approval processes.

Considerations: The vehicle is used as collateral, so the lender can repossess it if you default. Also, cars depreciate, so you could owe more than the car is worth (negative equity).

7. 401(k) Loan

Best For: Borrowing from yourself without applying for a traditional loan.

Where to Get It: Your own 401(k) retirement account, if your employer allows it.

Benefits:

No credit check required, and you pay interest back to your own retirement account.

Interest rates are usually lower than other loan types.

Considerations: You're borrowing against your retirement savings, which could impact your future financial security. If you leave your job, you may have to repay the loan in full or face taxes and penalties.

8. Microloans

Best For: Small businesses or entrepreneurs, especially those who are underserved by traditional banks.

Where to Get It: Microfinance institutions or organizations like Kiva, Accion, or Grameen Bank.

Benefits:

Accessible for those with limited credit history.

Smaller amounts are available, which is ideal for small-scale business needs.

Considerations: Loans are typically smaller (up to $50,000), and interest rates may be higher compared to traditional loans.

9. Payday Alternative Loans (PALs)

Best For: Short-term borrowing needs with a small loan amount, as an alternative to payday loans.

Where to Get It: Federal credit unions.

Benefits:

Much lower interest rates than payday loans.

Fixed fees and repayment terms (up to 6 months), avoiding the cycle of debt.

Considerations: Limited to credit union members, and loan amounts are usually small.

10. Student Loans

Best For: Financing education or student-related expenses.

Where to Get It: Federal government (for federal loans) or private lenders (for private loans).

Benefits:

Federal student loans offer lower interest rates, flexible repayment options, and deferment benefits.

Can help build credit if repaid responsibly.

Considerations: Private loans may have higher interest rates and fewer repayment options. Student debt can accumulate quickly, and deferment may delay, but not eliminate, repayment.

11. Credit Union Loans

Best For: Borrowers looking for lower interest rates and personalized service.

Where to Get It: Credit unions (member-owned financial cooperatives).

Benefits:

Often lower interest rates and fees than traditional banks.

More flexibility with loan terms and approval, especially for members.

Considerations: You must be a member of the credit union, and loan amounts may be limited.

12. Crowdfunding

Best For: Entrepreneurs, small businesses, or creative projects that need funding.

Where to Get It: Platforms like Kickstarter, GoFundMe, or Indiegogo.

Benefits:

No need to repay the money raised, as it's typically considered a donation or investment.

Offers marketing exposure and validation of ideas.

Considerations: There's no guarantee of reaching your fundraising goal, and some platforms charge fees.

Key Considerations When Borrowing

Credit Score: Your credit score impacts the interest rate and terms you'll receive. Higher credit scores generally lead to better borrowing terms.

Interest Rates: Always compare the APR (Annual Percentage Rate) between lenders to find the most cost-effective loan.

Repayment Terms: Understand the repayment schedule and if there are any penalties for early repayment.

Fees and Penalties: Be aware of any origination fees, late fees, or prepayment penalties that may apply.

Collateral: Secured loans (e.g., mortgages, auto loans) use collateral, while unsecured loans (e.g., personal loans, credit cards) do not. Secured loans usually have lower interest rates but higher risk if you default.

Borrowing from a cash value life insurance policy, such as a whole life or universal life policy, and Indexed Universal Life policies are a way to access the accumulated cash value without going through traditional lenders. Here's a step-by-step guide on how to borrow from your cash value life insurance policy.

1. Check Policy Type

Ensure you have a cash value life insurance policy (like whole life, universal life, or indexed universal life).

Term life insurance does not accumulate cash value, so loans are not possible with term policies.

2. Understand the Cash Value

Cash Value: This is the amount of money that accumulates in your life insurance policy over time. Part of your premiums goes into this cash value account.

Check how much cash value has accumulated in your policy, as this will determine how much you can borrow.

The loan amount is typically limited to a percentage of the total cash value, often around 80-90%.

3. Review the Policy Terms

Contact your insurance provider or read through your policy documents to understand the loan terms, including:

Interest Rate: Know the interest rate you'll be charged on the loan, which is typically lower than traditional loan rates.

Repayment Terms: While life insurance policy loans don't require regular payments, you can choose to repay it over time or not at all.

Impact on Death Benefit: The outstanding loan balance and any unpaid interest will reduce the death benefit paid to your beneficiaries.

4. Contact Your Insurance Provider

Reach out to your insurance company to request a loan from the cash value.

You can typically request the loan online, by phone, or by filling out a loan form.

The insurance provider will calculate how much you can borrow based on your cash value and policy terms.

5. Understand the Loan Interest

The loan will accrue interest, either at a fixed or variable rate, depending on your policy.

Some policies allow you to choose whether the interest is paid out of pocket or deducted from the remaining cash value.

If you don't pay back the loan or the interest, it will continue to compound, reducing your cash value and the death benefit.

6. No Credit Check or Approval Process

Since you are borrowing against your own money, there is no need for a credit check, approval process, or lengthy paperwork like with a traditional loan.

This makes it a quick and convenient option for borrowing.

7. Receive Funds

Once the loan is approved, the insurance company will disburse the funds to you, usually via direct deposit or check.

8. Repayment Options

Flexible Repayment: You can choose to repay the loan at your own pace, or not at all. Unlike traditional loans, there is no strict repayment schedule.

If you choose not to repay the loan, it will continue to accrue interest, and the unpaid balance will be deducted from your death benefit.

However, if the loan plus interest exceeds the cash value, the policy could lapse, meaning the policy will be canceled, and you may face tax implications.

9. Tax Implications

Loans from life insurance are generally tax-free as long as the policy remains in force.

However, if the policy lapses while there is an outstanding loan, the loan amount may become taxable as income.

10. Monitor the Policy

Keep track of your loan and the cash value balance to ensure you don't borrow too much and risk the policy lapsing.

Regularly review your statements to understand the impact of the loan on the policy's value and death benefit.

Key Considerations

Loan vs. Withdrawal: A loan allows you to borrow money against the policy's cash value without permanently reducing it. A withdrawal reduces the cash value and may decrease the policy's death benefit.

No Mandatory Repayment: You don't have to repay the loan, but unpaid interest will accrue, and the loan will be deducted from your death benefit.

Policy Lapse Risk: If the loan plus interest exceeds the cash value, your policy could lapse, leading to loss of coverage and potential tax consequences.

<u>Quiz</u>

1. How did Zoey develop a solid business plan before borrowing money, and what can you learn from her careful approach to ensure that the borrowed capital would be used effectively for business growth?

   ____

   ____

2. What strategies did Zoey use to balance her borrowed funds between launching her business, making investments, and managing personal debt, and how can these strategies help you manage your finances when starting a business?

   ____

   ____

3. How did Zoey's decision to invest in her business and make smart financial choices, such as paying off high-interest debts first, contribute to her long-term success, and what can be learned from her approach to achieving financial stability?

   ____

   ____

Retirement

On his bunk in deep thought, Benjamin was already thinking about his future. While his friends were more focused on the present, he couldn't shake the feeling that he needed to start planning for retirement sooner rather than later. He had a stable job in IT, but he knew that relying solely on his salary and a basic 401(k) wouldn't be enough to provide the comfortable retirement he envisioned. He wanted more—something that could generate long-term growth and create a source of supplemental income.

Discovering the Power of Compound Interest

One day, Benjamin met with a financial advisor who introduced him to the idea of compound interest—the concept of earning interest not just on the initial investment but also on the interest that accrues over time. Benjamin realized that this was the key to growing his wealth exponentially. He needed a financial vehicle that offered high returns and would allow him to take full advantage of compound interest over the years.

After researching his options, Benjamin chose to invest in a high-interest index fund. The fund tracked a broad range of stocks, offering a balance of growth and stability. With historically strong returns and the ability to reinvest dividends, this type of investment was ideal for his long-term strategy. He started contributing regularly, setting aside 15% of his income each month.

Creating Supplemental Income for Retirement

In addition to his retirement investments, Benjamin wanted to create supplemental income streams that would give him more financial freedom later in life. His financial advisor suggested using a fixed annuity as a part of his portfolio. A fixed annuity offered guaranteed payments during retirement and had the potential for high compound interest if left to grow over time.

Benjamin started funding his fixed annuity alongside his index fund investments. His plan was simple: let the annuity build for several decades and then convert it into a steady income stream when he retired. The high compound interest rates on both his index funds and annuity gave him confidence that his investments would generate significant returns over time.

Consistency and Patience Pay Off

Over the next 20 years, Benjamin remained disciplined. He contributed to his index fund and annuity consistently, reinvesting dividends and allowing compound interest to work its magic. While there were moments of market volatility, he trusted the long-term growth potential of his investments.

By the time Benjamin turned 55, his financial plan had paid off. His index fund had grown significantly, thanks to years of compound interest, and his annuity was fully funded. He was now in a position where his retirement savings were not only substantial, but they also had the potential to continue growing even after he stopped working.

Supplemental Income in Retirement

When Benjamin decided to retire at 60, he converted his annuity into monthly payments. This provided him with a steady stream of supplemental income on top of his 401(k) and Social Security benefits. The income from his annuity meant he didn't have to dip into his savings too early, allowing his investments to continue growing.

In addition to the annuity, the compound interest on his index fund had created a large nest egg. Benjamin could comfortably withdraw a portion of these funds each year without worrying about running out of money, thanks to the continuous growth fueled by compound interest. The combination of his annuity and the returns from his investments provided him with more than enough income to maintain his desired lifestyle.

The Long-Term Impact

Benjamin's early decision to invest in financial vehicles that leveraged high compound interest rates had completely changed his financial trajectory. He wasn't just scraping by in retirement—he was thriving. The supplemental income he had created allowed him to travel, enjoy hobbies, and even support his grandchildren's college education.

Reflecting on his journey, Benjamin realized that the power of compound interest, combined with the right financial vehicles, had set him up for long-term success. He had started early, stayed disciplined, and now, in retirement, he was reaping the rewards of his careful planning and smart investment choices.

A Comfortable, Secure Future

Thanks to his decision to focus on investments with high compound interest, Benjamin had built a future of financial security. His retirement was no longer a source of worry but a time of freedom and opportunity. The combination of his annuity and index fund provided him with a stable, growing income, ensuring he could enjoy the retirement he had always envisioned.

Are you prepared to retire? Have you planned it out effectively? Well creating a successful way to provide supplemental income for someone nearing retirement involves a blend of low-risk investments, part-time work, and leveraging existing assets. Here's a step-by-step guide that can help provide steady supplemental income without jeopardizing financial security in retirement.

1. Invest in Dividend-Paying Stocks

Best For: Generating regular passive income.

How It Works: Invest in blue-chip stocks or dividend-paying ETFs (Exchange-Traded Funds) that provide quarterly dividends. Dividends can provide a reliable income stream without needing to sell your investments.

Benefits:

Steady cash flow.

Potential for capital appreciation.

Considerations: While dividends are generally stable, they're not guaranteed, and the stock market is subject to volatility. However, long-term investments in solid companies tend to provide consistent returns.

2. Create a Rental Income Stream

Best For: Those who already own a home or can invest in real estate.

How It Works: Rent out a part of your home (like a basement apartment or spare room) or invest in rental properties that generate a monthly income stream.

Benefits:

Consistent monthly income.

Long-term real estate appreciation.

Considerations: Being a landlord requires management, upkeep, and potential dealing with tenants. Hiring a property manager can reduce these responsibilities, but it comes with additional costs.

3. Build a Side Business or Freelance Service

Best For: Retirees with skills that can be monetized.

How It Works: Leverage your professional expertise, hobbies, or passions to create a small side business or freelance service. Examples include:

Consulting in your field of expertise.

Freelancing as a writer, accountant, or designer.

Tutoring or teaching online.

Selling handmade products on platforms like Etsy.

Benefits:

Flexible hours and control over workload.

Low startup costs, especially with online freelancing or consulting.

Considerations: May require initial time and effort to establish, but it provides flexible income on your terms.

4. Set Up an Annuity

Best For: Those seeking guaranteed income.

How It Works: An annuity is a financial product that provides guaranteed regular payments in exchange for an upfront investment. This can act like a pension by providing monthly payments for a set period or even for life.

Benefits:

Predictable, steady income for life or a specified time.

Tax-deferred growth.

Considerations: Annuities can have high fees, and you may lose access to your principal investment. It's important to compare annuity products to find the best fit for your retirement goals.

5. Invest in Bonds or Bond Funds

Best For: Lower-risk, steady income.

How It Works: Buy government or corporate bonds that pay interest (coupons) over a fixed period. You can also invest in bond ETFs or mutual funds, which diversify across many bonds for lower risk.

Benefits:

Safe and predictable income stream.

Less volatility than stocks.

Considerations: Bonds generally provide lower returns compared to stocks, but they are safer and more stable.

6. Leverage a Reverse Mortgage

Best For: Retirees who own their home and need extra income.

How It Works: A reverse mortgage allows you to borrow against the equity in your home while continuing to live there. Payments are received either as a lump sum, monthly payments, or a line of credit, and the loan is repaid when the home is sold (typically after the homeowner passes away or moves).

Benefits:

Provides income without needing to sell or leave the home.

Can be a steady income source.

Considerations: This reduces the equity in your home, and if you want to leave the property to heirs, it may complicate their inheritance. Also, fees can be high.

7. Monetize Hobbies or Passions

Best For: Retirees with a strong hobby or creative talent.

How It Works: Turn a hobby or passion into a small business. Examples include:

Photography, painting, or craft-making can be sold on websites like Etsy or at local markets.

Writing a blog or self-publishing eBooks.

Gardening and selling produce at a local farmer's market.

Benefits:

Doing something enjoyable while generating income.

Flexible and low pressure.

Considerations: Monetizing a hobby can take time and may not generate significant income right away, but it can be rewarding personally and financially.

8. Take on a Part-Time Job

Best For: Those who want a structured way to supplement income.

How It Works: Look for part-time or seasonal jobs in fields you enjoy, such as:

Retail work, especially during busy seasons.

Driving for rideshare services (Uber, Lyft) or delivering groceries/food (DoorDash, Instacart).

Working at a local library, museum, or community center.

Benefits:

Provides extra income while keeping you active and engaged.

Can offer additional benefits like discounts or social connections.

Considerations: While part-time jobs are more flexible than full-time work, they still require time commitment and may limit your free time.

9. Sell or Rent Out Personal Assets

Best For: Immediate short-term income.

How It Works: Sell items you no longer need or rent out assets like:

Renting out vehicles (on platforms like Turo).

Selling collectibles, antiques, or furniture online.

Renting out tools, sports equipment, or even storage space through platforms like Neighbor.

Benefits:

Quick cash for items you no longer use.

Little to no long-term commitment.

Considerations: Income from selling assets is finite, and renting out assets may come with some maintenance or management.

10. Explore Affiliate Marketing or Content Creation

Best For: Retirees who enjoy writing or creating content.

How It Works: Create a blog, YouTube channel, or social media presence focused on a specific niche. By promoting products or services through affiliate links, you can earn commissions when others make purchases through your links.

Benefits:

Potential for passive income.

Low initial investment.

Considerations: It takes time to build an audience and see results, and success depends on consistent content creation.

Key Considerations for Creating Supplemental Income:

Diversification: Spread your income streams across different sources (e.g., investments, part-time work, real estate) to reduce risk.

Risk Tolerance: Choose income sources that match your risk tolerance, particularly as you near or enter retirement.

Time Commitment: Be mindful of how much time and effort you want to dedicate to earning supplemental income, balancing leisure with financial needs.

Longevity: Ensure that your supplemental income strategy can sustain you for the long term and support your lifestyle through your retirement years.

Quiz

1. How did Benjamin's early understanding of compound interest influence his decision to invest in high-interest financial vehicles, and what can be learned from his long-term approach to growing wealth for retirement?

   ____

   ____

2. What steps did Benjamin take to diversify his investments, such as choosing both an index fund and a fixed annuity, and how did this strategy provide him with both growth and supplemental income in retirement?

   ____

   ____

3. How did Benjamin's consistent contributions and disciplined investment approach over 20 years prepare him for a comfortable retirement, and what key practices can others adopt to ensure similar financial success?

   ____

   ____

Investing

Mila had tried investing several times in her late twenties, but each attempt ended in frustration. She had jumped into stocks without much research, chased quick profits, and lost more than she gained. By the time she turned 33, she was ready to give up.

One evening, a friend suggested she take a step back and really learn the basics. Mila decided to start small, investing in a diversified index fund and focusing on long-term growth. This time, she was patient and consistent, letting her investments grow steadily.

By 36, Mila was finally seeing success. Her portfolio had grown, and she had learned that investing wasn't about quick wins—it was about smart, steady decisions over time.

Now you are ready to start investing. Creating a safe and successful investment strategy involves balancing risk with potential reward, while focusing on long-term financial growth and security. Below is a guide for someone looking to invest safely while still aiming for reasonable returns:

1. Build a Solid Financial Foundation First

Emergency Fund: Before you invest, make sure you have at least 3-6 months' worth of living expenses in an easily accessible savings account. This acts as a safety net in case of unexpected expenses, preventing you from having to sell investments prematurely.

Pay Off High-Interest Debt: Prioritize paying off any high-interest debts (like credit cards) before investing. The interest you save on debt often outweighs investment returns.

2. Invest in a Diverse Portfolio of Low-Risk Assets

Diversification is key to reducing risk while investing. By spreading your investments across different asset classes, you limit the impact of any one investment performing poorly.

A. Bonds & Bond Funds

Best For: Steady, lower-risk returns.

What It Is: Bonds are loans you give to the government or corporations, and they pay you interest over time.

Where to Invest: U.S. Treasury bonds, corporate bonds, or municipal bonds. You can also invest in bond funds or ETFs (Exchange-Traded Funds) for added diversification.

Why It's Safe: Bonds are generally safer than stocks, especially U.S. Treasury bonds, which are backed by the government.

B. Dividend-Paying Stocks or ETFs

Best For: Generating passive income with moderate risk.

What It Is: Dividend-paying stocks are shares of companies that distribute part of their profits to shareholders in the form of dividends. Dividend-focused ETFs spread your money across multiple dividend-paying companies.

Where to Invest: Focus on blue-chip companies (well-established, financially sound companies with reliable dividend histories) or dividend-focused ETFs like Vanguard Dividend Appreciation ETF (VIG).

Why It's Safe: Dividends provide a consistent income stream, and blue-chip companies tend to be more stable.

C. Index Funds and ETFs

Best For: Long-term, low-cost growth with broad diversification.

What It Is: Index funds and ETFs track the performance of a specific market index (e.g., the S&P 500), giving you exposure to a wide variety of stocks at a low cost.

Where to Invest: Popular index funds/ETFs include Vanguard S&P 500 ETF (VOO) and Fidelity Zero Total Market Index Fund (FZROX).

Why It's Safe: Index funds and ETFs spread your risk across hundreds or thousands of companies, making it less likely that poor performance from one company will significantly affect your portfolio.

D. High-Interest Savings Accounts or CDs

Best For: Preserving capital with no risk.

What It Is: High-yield savings accounts or Certificates of Deposit (CDs) offer a risk-free way to earn a modest return on your savings.

Where to Invest: Online banks like Ally or Marcus by Goldman Sachs often offer competitive interest rates.

Why It's Safe: These are FDIC-insured, meaning your money is protected up to $250,000 per depositor, per bank.

3. Use Dollar-Cost Averaging

What It Is: Dollar-cost averaging (DCA) is an investment strategy where you invest a fixed amount of money at regular intervals (e.g., monthly or quarterly), regardless of market conditions.

Why It's Safe: DCA reduces the risk of investing a large amount of money right before a market drop, and it smooths out the purchase price of investments over time.

Example: Instead of investing $10,000 all at once, invest $1,000 each month over 10 months. This helps mitigate the risk of market timing and ensures you buy more shares when prices are low and fewer shares when prices are high.

4. Invest in Retirement Accounts (Tax-Advantaged)

Best For: Long-term growth and tax benefits.

What It Is: Retirement accounts like a 401(k), IRA, or Roth IRA offer tax advantages that can significantly increase your long-term returns.

Where to Invest:

401(k): If your employer offers a 401(k), contribute at least enough to get the full employer match (if available).

IRA/Roth IRA: Open an IRA or Roth IRA for additional retirement savings. In a Roth IRA, your contributions grow tax-free, and you don't pay taxes on withdrawals in retirement.

Why It's Safe: Investing in retirement accounts benefits from tax advantages, and you have decades to ride out market fluctuations. You can invest in a mix of index funds, bonds, and other assets within these accounts to tailor your risk level.

5. Automate Your Investments

What It Is: Set up automatic contributions to your investment accounts (e.g., 401(k), IRA, brokerage account).

Why It's Safe: Automation ensures that you consistently invest without trying to time the market. It also helps you build wealth steadily over time without emotional interference.

6. Rebalance Your Portfolio Regularly

What It Is: Over time, some investments will grow faster than others, shifting your portfolio's risk level. Rebalancing involves periodically adjusting your portfolio back to your original asset allocation.

Why It's Safe: Rebalancing helps you maintain the right level of risk based on your investment goals and timeline. It prevents your portfolio from becoming overly risky due to an overweight in stocks after a market run-up.

7. Consider Low-Risk Real Estate Investments

Best For: Generating income with moderate risk.

What It Is: Real estate can offer passive income through real estate investment trusts (REITs) or rental properties.

Where to Invest:

REITs: REITs are companies that own or finance income-producing real estate. You can invest in REITs through the stock market or ETFs, like Vanguard Real Estate ETF (VNQ).

Rental Properties: Buying a rental property can generate monthly income through rent, though it comes with more active management.

Why It's Safe: REITs allow you to invest in real estate without needing to manage property directly. They also tend to offer reliable income through dividends. Rental properties can provide a steady income stream if managed properly.

8. Keep Investment Costs Low

Why It's Important: High fees can eat into your returns over time, so it's crucial to invest in low-cost options like index funds or ETFs.

How to Do It: Choose funds with low expense ratios (below 0.5%) and avoid high-cost mutual funds or actively managed funds unless they consistently outperform their benchmarks.

9. Stay Patient and Focus on the Long Term

What It Is: Successful investing is not about getting rich quickly. The key to safe investing is to focus on long-term growth, avoiding emotional reactions to short-term market fluctuations.

Why It's Safe: Time in the market is more important than timing the market. Historically, markets trend upward over the long run, so staying invested through market ups and downs generally leads to success.

Example of a Safe Investment Portfolio:

40% in a mix of U.S. Treasury bonds or bond ETFs.

30% in a broad-market index fund (like the S&P 500).

15% in dividend-paying stocks or dividend-focused ETFs.

10% in a real estate ETF (REIT).

5% in a high-interest savings account or CD for short-term liquidity.

Quiz

How does focusing on long-term growth, like Mila's approach with diversified index funds, lead to more consistent success compared to chasing quick profits?

____

____

What lessons can be learned from Mila's early investment failures, and how important is research and patience when starting your investment journey?

____

____

How can diversifying your portfolio help mitigate risks and increase the chances of long-term success in investing?

____

____

Taxes

For the record, we are not a tax professional so some of the amounts shown in this next guide can change based on your location and the time you purchased this book. Amounts can be greater or less depending on the state in which you live in. To leverage tax loopholes, perks, and legal strategies to reduce your tax liability, it's essential to understand tax law fundamentals, business deductions, and available credits. Below is a strategic guide to help you utilize tax loopholes and perks while writing off expenses, focused on maximizing savings without breaking the law.

1. Set Up a Business or Side Hustle

Why It Works: By setting up a business, even a small side hustle, you can access a wide range of deductions and write-offs for business-related expenses.

How to Do It: Start a small business as a sole proprietor, LLC, or S-Corp. Keep detailed records of all business-related expenses and income.

What You Can Write Off: Business-related expenses like office supplies, utilities, equipment, travel, meals, marketing, and more.

Example Write-Offs:

Home Office Deduction: If you run a business from home, you can deduct a portion of your rent/mortgage, utilities, and internet based on the square footage of your office space. It can be calculated as a simplified deduction (up to $1,500 annually) or a more complex formula involving exact percentages.

Business Meals: Deduct 50% of meals you buy for business purposes, like meeting clients or discussing business with colleagues.

Vehicle Expenses: Deduct either the mileage (set rate by the IRS, such as $0.655 per mile for 2023) or actual expenses (gas, repairs, insurance) for business travel.

2. Utilize Retirement Accounts for Tax Deferral

Why It Works: Contributions to tax-advantaged retirement accounts reduce your taxable income, potentially saving you thousands of dollars in taxes.

How to Do It: Maximize contributions to 401(k), Traditional IRA, SEP IRA, or Solo 401(k) if you are self-employed.

Key Benefits:

401(k) Contributions: The contribution limit for 2024 is $23,000 (plus a $7,500 catch-up contribution if you're 50 or older). Contributions reduce your taxable income and grow tax-deferred.

SEP IRA/Solo 401(k): For self-employed individuals, these accounts allow higher contribution limits (up to 25% of your net earnings or $66,000 for 2023).

Health Savings Account (HSA): If you have a high-deductible health plan, contribute to an HSA, where contributions are tax-deductible, growth is tax-free, and withdrawals for qualified medical expenses are tax-free.

3. Take Advantage of Depreciation

Why It Works: Depreciation allows you to deduct the cost of an asset over its useful life, reducing taxable income. With the introduction of bonus depreciation and Section 179 expensing, you can accelerate these deductions.

How to Do It: Purchase business-related assets like vehicles, machinery, or property. Under current tax laws, you can deduct 100% bonus depreciation in the year the asset is placed in service (2023) or use Section 179 to deduct up to $1,160,000 for business equipment.

Example: If you buy a $50,000 business vehicle, you can immediately deduct the full cost under bonus depreciation, reducing your tax liability by that amount in the current tax year.

4. Tax-Free Fringe Benefits

Why It Works: Certain fringe benefits provided by an employer (including self-employment) are not taxable to employees but are deductible for the employer, reducing overall taxable income.

How to Do It: Offer tax-free fringe benefits to yourself or employees through your business.

Key Benefits:

Health Insurance: Premiums paid by your business for your health insurance are tax-deductible, and the benefit is tax-free to you.

Educational Assistance: Provide up to $5,250 per year in tax-free educational assistance for employees, including yourself if you're self-employed.

Commuter Benefits: Provide tax-free commuter benefits for parking, public transportation, or even bike commuting.

Retirement Matching: If your business offers a 401(k) match, the matching contributions are tax-deductible for the business but tax-deferred for employees.

5. Leverage Real Estate Tax Strategies

Why It Works: Real estate investments offer significant tax benefits through depreciation, mortgage interest deductions, and special strategies like 1031 exchanges.

How to Do It: Invest in rental properties or commercial real estate and use the following strategies:

Key Tax Perks:

Mortgage Interest Deduction: Deduct mortgage interest paid on rental properties, reducing taxable income.

Depreciation: Deduct the cost of the property over 27.5 years (for residential) or 39 years (for commercial), reducing your taxable rental income.

1031 Exchange: Defer capital gains taxes by using the proceeds from selling a property to reinvest in another "like-kind" property within a specified timeframe.

Short-Term Rentals: If you rent out part of your primary home or a vacation home for less than 14 days a year, you can collect rental income tax-free.

6. Deduct Travel Expenses for Business or Investment Purposes

Why It Works: If you travel for business or to manage an investment property, these expenses are deductible.

How to Do It: Ensure the primary purpose of the trip is business-related. You can deduct airfare, hotel, meals, car rentals, and other travel-related expenses.

Key Tip: If you mix business and leisure, you can still deduct the business portion. For example, if you spend 4 days working and 2 days vacationing, you can write off most of the travel and accommodation expenses as long as the primary purpose was business.

7. Optimize Capital Gains and Losses (Tax-Loss Harvesting)

Why It Works: Capital gains are taxed at a lower rate than ordinary income, and you can use capital losses to offset gains or reduce your taxable income by up to $3,000 per year.

How to Do It: Time your stock or asset sales to take advantage of long-term capital gains rates (for assets held more than a year), and use losses from underperforming investments to offset your gains.

Key Strategies:

Long-Term vs. Short-Term Gains: Long-term capital gains (held for over 12 months) are taxed at a lower rate (0%, 15%, or 20%), while short-term gains are taxed at your ordinary income tax rate.

Tax-Loss Harvesting: Sell underperforming stocks to realize losses and offset your capital gains. You can use up to $3,000 of excess losses to offset ordinary income.

8. Maximize Tax Credits

Why It Works: Tax credits reduce your tax liability dollar-for-dollar, making them more valuable than deductions. Some credits are even refundable, meaning you can receive a refund if they exceed your tax liability.

How to Do It: Claim available credits for which you qualify, such as the Earned Income Tax Credit, Child Tax Credit, Residential Energy Credits, and more.

Key Tax Credits:

Earned Income Tax Credit (EITC): A refundable credit for low- to moderate-income earners. You can get a significant refund even if you owe no taxes.

Child Tax Credit: Up to $2,000 per child, and up to $1,500 may be refundable if your tax liability is zero.

Education Credits: The American Opportunity Credit offers up to $2,500 per student, while the Lifetime Learning Credit offers up to $2,000 for education-related expenses.

Residential Energy Credits: Claim credits for installing solar panels, energy-efficient windows, or other renewable energy systems on your property.

9. Strategic Charitable Contributions

Why It Works: Charitable contributions are tax-deductible, and with proper planning, you can maximize their impact while reducing your tax liability.

How to Do It: Donate cash, goods, or stocks to qualified charities, and itemize your deductions to take advantage of the write-off.

Key Tip:

Donate Appreciated Assets: Instead of selling stocks and donating the cash, donate the stock itself. You avoid capital gains tax on the appreciated value and can still deduct the full market value of the asset, maximizing your tax benefit.

10. Hire Your Family for Business Purposes

Why It Works: Hiring your family, such as your spouse or children, for legitimate business work allows you to deduct their wages as a business expense.

How to Do It: Pay reasonable wages for work done, and ensure the job is legitimate (e.g., office assistant, website maintenance).

Key Perk: If you hire your child under 18 and operate as a sole proprietorship or LLC, you don't have to pay Social Security or Medicare taxes on their wages, creating even more savings.

11. Leverage the S-Corp Tax Election

Why It Works: S-Corporations allow you to save on self-employment taxes by paying yourself a reasonable salary and taking the remaining profits as distributions.

How to Do It: File an election for S-Corp status for your LLC or corporation. Pay yourself a salary (which is subject to payroll taxes) and take distributions, which are not subject to self-employment tax.

Example: If your business profits are $100,000, you could pay yourself a $50,000 salary (subject to payroll taxes) and take the remaining $50,000 as distributions (not subject to self-employment taxes), saving thousands in taxes.

Conclusion

This comprehensive tax strategy enables you to leverage legal tax loopholes and perks, minimize taxable income through business-related write-offs, and maximize retirement savings and investment gains. Be sure to consult with a tax professional to ensure compliance and tailor strategies to your unique situation.

Compound Interest

David was feeling overwhelmed by his finances, aware that he had a stable job but was struggling to save for the future. One day, while researching retirement options, he stumbled upon the concept of cash value life insurance and its potential for compound interest.

Intrigued, David met with a financial advisor who explained how cash value accounts work. He learned that as he paid premiums, a portion of that money would accumulate cash value over time, earning interest that compounds. Excited by the prospect, he decided to open a cash value life insurance policy.

David committed to contributing regularly, treating it like a forced savings account. Over the years, he watched as his cash value grew steadily. By the time he turned 40, the account had accumulated a significant amount, providing him with not just a safety net but also a valuable asset for future investments.

With the power of compound interest working in his favor, David finally felt confident about his financial future. He realized that starting early and making informed decisions had transformed his approach to savings and investing, setting him up for long-term success.

For the purpose of utilizing compound interest effectively can significantly grow your wealth over time. The key to maximizing its power is choosing the right financial vehicles and strategies that offer high interest returns. Below is a strategy to harness compound interest, followed by a list of the best financial vehicles available for high returns.

1. Understanding Compound Interest

Compound Interest Formula:

A=P(1+nr)nt

A = the future value of the investment/loan, including interest

P = the principal investment amount

r = the annual interest rate (decimal)

n = the number of times interest is compounded per year

t = the number of years the money is invested or borrowed for

How It Works: Compound interest earns interest on both the initial principal and the accumulated interest from previous periods. The more frequent the compounding (daily, monthly, quarterly, annually), the faster your money grows.

2. Strategies for Maximizing Compound Interest

a. Start Early

Why It Works: Time is the most critical factor for compound interest. The earlier you start investing, the more time your money has to grow.

Example: Investing $5,000 at an 8% return for 40 years will yield significantly more than investing the same amount for only 20 years, even if you invest larger amounts later in life.

b. Contribute Regularly

Why It Works: Regular contributions, whether weekly, monthly, or annually, increase the amount of money compounding over time.

How to Do It: Set up automatic transfers to investment accounts to consistently add funds.

c. Reinvest Dividends and Interest

Why It Works: Reinvesting dividends and interest allows those returns to compound further, accelerating the growth of your investments.

How to Do It: Opt for dividend reinvestment plans (DRIPs) or automatically reinvest interest from bonds and other fixed-income securities.

d. Choose High-Interest, Low-Risk Vehicles

Why It Works: Higher interest rates lead to more significant compounding effects, but balance this with risk tolerance and diversification.

How to Do It: Select a diversified portfolio of financial products that offer a solid return with minimal risk.

3. Best Financial Vehicles Offering High Interest Returns

a. Stocks and Exchange-Traded Funds (ETFs)

Why It Works: Historically, the stock market has returned an average of 7-10% annually, making it one of the best long-term investments for compound growth.

Key Vehicle:

Index Funds/ETFs: Invest in broad market indices like the S&P 500, which provides diversification and lower risk compared to individual stocks.

Dividend-Paying Stocks: Choose blue-chip companies with consistent dividends, and reinvest the dividends to harness compounding.

Example:

Vanguard Total Stock Market ETF (VTI) or SPDR S&P 500 ETF (SPY). Both offer exposure to hundreds of companies and have historically provided long-term growth around 7-8% annually.

b. High-Yield Savings Accounts (HYSA)

Why It Works: These accounts offer higher interest rates than traditional savings accounts, with some currently yielding between 4-5% annually.

Best for: Short-term savings, emergency funds, or money you may need to access quickly while still earning compound interest.

Key Options:

Marcus by Goldman Sachs: Currently offering a competitive rate around 4-5%.

Ally Bank: Known for its no-fee structure and high-yield savings options.

c. Certificates of Deposit (CDs)

Why It Works: CDs offer fixed, higher interest rates compared to savings accounts and are ideal for medium-term investments if you won't need the funds immediately.

Best for: Investors who want a guaranteed return without the risk of losing principal. Look for CDs with higher APYs and compare rates between banks.

Key Options:

Capital One 360: Offers CDs with rates ranging from 4-5% for longer terms (e.g., 5-year CDs).

Synchrony Bank: Offers competitive rates on 12-month to 60-month CDs.

d. Treasury Inflation-Protected Securities (TIPS)

Why It Works: TIPS provide interest payments that adjust with inflation, protecting the real value of your investment.

Best for: Conservative investors looking for inflation protection and steady, low-risk returns.

Key Feature: Interest is compounded semiannually and adjusted for inflation based on the Consumer Price Index (CPI).

e. Peer-to-Peer Lending Platforms

Why It Works: P2P lending platforms allow you to lend money directly to borrowers, often offering higher interest rates (5-12%) in exchange for moderate risk.

Best for: Investors looking to diversify their income streams and are comfortable with moderate risk.

Key Platforms:

LendingClub: Returns vary depending on the borrower's risk profile but can offer strong compounding if managed carefully.

Prosper: Offers similar peer-to-peer lending with an expected return between 5-10%.

f. Real Estate Investment Trusts (REITs)

Why It Works: REITs invest in income-producing real estate, paying out the majority of their earnings as dividends. These dividends can be reinvested, compounding your investment over time.

Best for: Investors looking for a mix of capital appreciation and steady income through dividends.

Key Options:

Vanguard Real Estate ETF (VNQ): Offers diversified exposure to real estate with historical dividend yields around 3-5%.

Fundrise: A platform for investing in private real estate with the potential for higher returns (8-12% on average).

g. Cryptocurrency (High Risk/High Reward)

Why It Works: Cryptocurrencies can offer astronomical returns, but they come with significant risk. Staking or earning interest on crypto holdings allows you to compound returns.

Best for: Investors with a high risk tolerance seeking potentially high rewards.

Key Platforms:

BlockFi (or similar platforms): Earn interest by lending out your cryptocurrency (rates vary, but can be as high as 5-8% for stablecoins).

Coinbase Staking: Offers rewards for staking certain cryptocurrencies like Ethereum (ETH) and Solana (SOL), with returns ranging from 4-8%.

4. Additional Strategies to Maximize Compound Interest

a. Increase Contributions Over Time

Why It Works: As your income grows, gradually increasing your contributions will accelerate the compounding process.

How to Do It: If you receive a raise or bonus, increase the percentage of your income that goes into high-yield savings, retirement accounts, or investments.

b. Tax-Advantaged Accounts

Why It Works: Contributing to tax-deferred accounts like 401(k), Traditional IRA, or tax-free accounts like a Roth IRA allows your investments to grow without being reduced by annual taxes.

Best for: Long-term investors seeking to minimize taxes on compounded gains.

Key Accounts:

401(k): Contributions are tax-deferred, allowing your investments to grow unhindered by taxes until withdrawal.

Roth IRA: Contributions are made with after-tax dollars, but all future growth and withdrawals are tax-free.

Health Savings Account (HSA): Contributions are tax-deductible, grow tax-free, and withdrawals for qualified medical expenses are tax-free, making it a powerful triple-tax-advantaged account.

c. Automate and Set It and Forget It

Why It Works: Automating your investments ensures consistent contributions without emotional decision-making, allowing compound interest to work uninterrupted.

How to Do It: Set up automatic contributions into your investment accounts, and avoid frequent buying and selling, which can disrupt the compounding process.

Conclusion

To maximize compound interest, start early, contribute regularly, reinvest earnings, and choose high-interest financial vehicles like stocks/ETFs, high-yield savings, CDs, REITs, and cryptocurrency **(if you're comfortable with risk).** Combine these strategies with tax-advantaged accounts like Roth IRAs, 401(k)s, and HSAs to allow your money to grow without being eroded by taxes, and leverage the power of compound interest over the long term for significant wealth accumulation.

Quiz

How can starting early with compound interest, like David did with his cash value account, maximize your long-term financial growth, and why is it important to begin as soon as possible?

____

____

What are some common mistakes to avoid when relying on compound interest, such as inconsistent contributions or withdrawing funds too early, that could disrupt the growth of your investments?

____

____

How does selecting the right financial vehicle, like a cash value account or high-interest savings plan, affect your ability to fully leverage compound interest, and what should you avoid when choosing an option?

____

____

Credit

Here is a story about Timothy, at 25, knew he wanted to build something big—his own business. But with limited savings and no credit history, his options were slim. Determined, he started by building his personal credit. He got a secured credit card, paid off the balance in full every month, and over the next two years, saw his credit score steadily rise.

With strong personal credit, Timothy then focused on establishing business credit. He registered his business, opened a business bank account, and took out small business loans, making sure to repay them on time. This helped him build a solid business credit profile.

By 30, Timothy had excellent credit on both fronts. He leveraged his personal and business credit to secure a large loan and purchased a few lucrative assets, including rental properties and equipment for his business. These assets generated passive income and helped his business thrive.

Through patience and smart credit management, Timothy turned his creditworthiness into a powerful tool for acquiring wealth, setting himself up for long-term success.

When Leveraging credit wisely it can be a powerful tool for generating long-term wealth if used responsibly. The key to success is managing your debt effectively while using borrowed funds to invest in income-generating or appreciating assets. Here's a comprehensive strategy on how to utilize credit and leverage it for investment purposes and long-term financial gains.

1. Build and Maintain a Strong Credit Score

Why It Matters: A strong credit score gives you access to lower interest rates, higher credit limits, and better terms when borrowing.

How to Do It:

Pay bills on time: Your payment history is the most significant factor in your credit score.

Keep credit utilization low: Aim to use less than 30% of your available credit.

Diversify credit types: Use a mix of credit cards, loans, and lines of credit responsibly.

Limit hard inquiries: Too many credit checks can temporarily lower your score.

Key Tip: Regularly monitor your credit report and score using free services like Credit Karma or through your bank.

2. Use Low-Interest Loans and Credit Lines for Investments

Why It Works: Borrowing at a low-interest rate to invest in assets that yield higher returns can create a positive arbitrage, where the returns on your investments exceed the cost of borrowing.

How to Do It:

Home Equity Line of Credit (HELOC): Use the equity in your home to secure a low-interest loan. HELOCs often offer interest rates around 4-6% and can be used for real estate investments, renovations, or even stock market investments.

Personal Loans: If you have strong credit, you can obtain personal loans with interest rates between 5-10%, which can be used for investment opportunities like real estate or business ventures.

Business Lines of Credit: If you're a business owner, a business line of credit offers flexible, low-cost borrowing to finance business growth or investments.

Example: If you secure a HELOC with a 5% interest rate and invest in real estate or a business venture yielding 8-12%, the difference in interest and return (3-7%) represents your profit from leveraging credit.

3. Leverage Credit for Real Estate Investing

Why It Works: Real estate is one of the most common assets leveraged through credit because of its potential for appreciation and cash flow through rental income.

How to Do It:

Traditional Mortgages: Use a mortgage to finance rental properties. With low-interest rates and tax-deductible interest, real estate can provide steady cash flow and appreciate over time.

FHA Loans: First-time homebuyers can use FHA loans with as little as 3.5% down to buy a property, live in one unit, and rent out the others to cover mortgage payments and generate passive income (house hacking).

BRRRR Method (Buy, Rehab, Rent, Refinance, Repeat): Buy distressed properties using credit, renovate them to increase value, rent them out, and then refinance to pull out the increased equity for future investments.

Key Tip: Ensure that the rental income from the property covers the mortgage, taxes, insurance, and other expenses to make the investment sustainable.

4. Use Credit Cards for Smart Investment Moves

Why It Works: When used strategically, credit cards with rewards, 0% APR offers, and cashback can be leveraged for financial gain. However, discipline is critical to avoid falling into high-interest debt.

How to Do It:

0% Intro APR Credit Cards: Many credit cards offer 0% interest on purchases or balance transfers for 12-18 months. You can use this interest-free period to fund small investments, pay for business startup costs, or consolidate high-interest debt without accruing interest.

Rewards and Cashback Cards: Use credit cards that offer rewards points, travel miles, or cashback on everyday spending. Accumulate points to reduce your overall expenses or reinvest the cashback into income-generating assets.

Example: Use a 0% APR credit card to finance the purchase of equipment for a small side business or rental property repairs. Pay off the balance before the promotional period ends, avoiding interest while generating income.

5. Leverage Margin for Stock Market Investments

Why It Works: Margin allows you to borrow money from your brokerage to invest in the stock market. By using margin, you can increase your purchasing power and potentially enhance returns.

How to Do It:

Open a Margin Account: With a margin account, your brokerage lends you money to purchase more stock than you could with your available cash.

Key Risks: Be cautious, as margin magnifies both gains and losses. If your investments decrease in value, you could face a margin call, requiring you to deposit more money or sell assets to cover the loan.

Example: If you have $10,000 in cash and borrow another $10,000 on margin to buy $20,000 worth of stock, a 10% gain would yield a $2,000 profit instead of $1,000. However, a 10% loss would double as well.

6. Invest in Income-Producing Assets Using Credit

Why It Works: Borrowing to invest in income-producing assets, such as rental properties, dividend stocks, or business ventures, can provide steady cash flow to pay off the debt and create long-term wealth.

How to Do It:

Real Estate: Use mortgage financing to purchase rental properties that generate monthly rental income. Ensure the property has positive cash flow, meaning rental income exceeds the mortgage payment and expenses.

Dividend Stocks: Use low-interest loans or credit lines to invest in dividend-paying stocks. Dividend income can be used to cover loan interest and build wealth through capital appreciation.

Franchise or Business Investment: Leverage a small business loan to buy or start a business that produces regular cash flow. Business earnings can be used to pay down debt while increasing equity.

Example: Purchase a rental property using a 75% loan-to-value (LTV) mortgage. If the rental property generates $2,000 in monthly rent and the mortgage payment is $1,500, you net $500 per month, which can be used to pay down the loan faster or invest elsewhere.

7. Utilize the Snowball or Avalanche Method to Manage Debt

Why It Works: Effective debt management ensures that your leveraged investments do not lead to overwhelming interest payments or financial strain. The snowball method focuses on paying off small debts first, while the avalanche method prioritizes high-interest debt.

How to Do It:

Snowball Method: Pay off the smallest debt first, then roll that payment into the next largest debt. This builds momentum and keeps motivation high.

Avalanche Method: Pay off the debt with the highest interest rate first to minimize overall interest payments and increase your long-term savings.

Key Tip: Whichever method you choose, ensure you avoid missing payments to protect your credit score and reduce penalties.

8. Invest in Yourself Using Credit

Why It Works: Investing in education, certifications, or skills development using low-interest loans or credit can significantly boost your earning potential, leading to higher income and more investment opportunities.

How to Do It:

Student Loans: Use student loans for professional education that has a high return on investment (e.g., medical, law, tech fields).

Business Loans: Take out loans to invest in skills, courses, or certifications that help you start or grow a profitable business.

Example: Use a personal loan to pay for an MBA or other professional certification. The increased earning potential from higher-paying job opportunities can offset the cost of the loan and accelerate your wealth-building efforts.

9. Use Credit to Scale Your Business

Why It Works: Scaling a business using credit allows you to grow faster by financing inventory, equipment, marketing, or expansion. If done correctly, the increased revenue will outweigh the cost of the debt.

How to Do It:

Business Credit Cards: Use a business credit card with rewards to cover operational costs. Pay the balance in full each month to avoid interest while earning points or cashback.

SBA Loans: Small Business Administration loans offer low-interest financing for growing or scaling a business.

Vendor Financing: Some vendors offer 30-90 day payment terms, allowing you to sell the inventory or services before paying for them, effectively creating a short-term, interest-free loan.

Example: Use a $50,000 SBA loan to open a second location of a profitable restaurant. The increased revenue covers the loan payments and allows you to reinvest profits into further growth.

10. Monitor and Adjust Your Leverage Ratio

Why It Works: Maintaining a healthy balance between debt and equity ensures you can weather downturns or unexpected expenses without becoming over-leveraged.

How to Do It:

Track Debt-to-Income (DTI) Ratio: Keep your DTI ratio (monthly debt payments divided by gross monthly income) below 35% for personal finances and under 50% for business leverage.

Adjust as Needed: If your investments perform well, you may be able to take on more leverage. If they underperform, focus on paying down debt and reducing risk.

Conclusion

Leveraging credit for investments can be a powerful strategy for wealth creation if done responsibly. By maintaining a strong credit score, using low-interest credit lines for income-generating investments, and managing debt effectively, you can multiply your investment gains while minimizing risks. Remember, the key is to use credit wisely, invest in assets that appreciate or produce income, and always ensure you can cover your debt obligations.

Quiz

How did Timothy's approach to building personal credit, such as using a secured credit card and making timely payments, help him establish a strong foundation for future financial opportunities?

____

____

What are the key steps Timothy took to build his business credit, and why is separating personal and business credit important when growing a business?

____

____

How can leveraging both personal and business credit, like Timothy did, help you acquire lucrative assets and grow wealth, and what are the risks if credit is mismanaged?

____

____

Emergency Fund

Sarah was living comfortably, enjoying her stable job and a good social life. She had enough to cover her bills and occasional splurges, but she had never prioritized saving for an emergency fund. "I'll start saving next month," she always told herself.

One day, unexpectedly, her car broke down, and the repair costs were steep. A week later, she learned her company was downsizing, and she lost her job. With no emergency fund, Sarah was forced to rely on credit cards, quickly racking up debt just to cover basic expenses.

Realizing her mistake, Sarah vowed to never be in this position again. Once she found a new job, she immediately started building an emergency fund. Slowly, she set aside a portion of each paycheck until she had enough to cover six months of living expenses.

Years later, when a similar crisis hit, Sarah was prepared. Her emergency fund gave her the peace of mind and financial cushion to handle the situation without falling into debt again. She learned that having an emergency fund wasn't just important—it was essential for financial security.

I believe that building a long-term emergency fund is essential for financial security, protecting you and your family from unexpected events like job loss, medical emergencies, or major repairs. A well-established emergency fund can prevent you from relying on credit or loans during tough times, ensuring long-term stability. Here's a step-by-step strategy for building a robust emergency fund.

1. Set a Clear Emergency Fund Goal

Why It Matters: Defining a target amount gives you a specific goal to work toward. Experts typically recommend saving 3-6 months' worth of living expenses, but your target may vary based on your personal situation.

How to Calculate:

Add up essential monthly expenses like rent/mortgage, utilities, groceries, transportation, and insurance.

Multiply by 3-6 months (or more if you have variable income or more dependents).

Consider factors like family size, job stability, and income variability.

Example: If your essential expenses total $3,000 per month, aim for a fund of $9,000 (3 months) to $18,000 (6 months). If you have a larger family or less job security, consider saving for 6-12 months of expenses.

2. Create a Budget and Identify Savings Opportunities

Why It Matters: A well-structured budget helps you track income and expenses, making it easier to find areas where you can save for your emergency fund.

How to Do It:

Track all income and expenses: Use a budgeting app like YNAB, Mint, or a simple spreadsheet to list income sources and regular expenses.

Identify areas to cut back: Look for non-essential spending (e.g., dining out, entertainment, subscriptions) and allocate that money to your emergency fund.

Automate Savings: Set up automatic transfers to a separate emergency fund account to ensure consistent contributions.

Key Tip: Even small, consistent savings can build up over time. If you save $200 per month, that's $2,400 in a year.

3. Prioritize High-Interest Debt Repayment First

Why It Matters: High-interest debt, like credit card debt, can erode your financial stability and slow down your ability to save. Paying it off first will free up more money for your emergency fund.

How to Do It:

Use the avalanche method to pay off the highest-interest debts first, while still making minimum payments on other debts.

Once high-interest debts are paid off, redirect those payments into your emergency fund.

Example: If you're paying $200 a month toward credit card debt, after paying it off, allocate that same amount to your emergency savings.

4. Open a Separate, High-Yield Savings Account

Why It Matters: Keeping your emergency fund separate from your regular checking account reduces the temptation to spend it. A high-yield savings account (HYSA) allows your savings to grow faster than in a traditional account.

How to Do It:

Choose a HYSA with a competitive interest rate (typically 3-5%).

Look for accounts with no fees, easy online access, and no minimum balance requirements.

Consider online banks like Ally Bank, Marcus by Goldman Sachs, or Capital One 360.

Example: If you save $10,000 in a high-yield account earning 4%, you'll earn $400 in interest annually—money that compounds and helps your emergency fund grow faster.

5. Establish Consistent Savings Habits

Why It Matters: Regularly contributing to your emergency fund ensures steady progress. Even small amounts saved consistently can accumulate into a significant sum over time.

How to Do It:

Start small: If saving a large amount seems overwhelming, start with manageable goals like $20 or $50 per week.

Increase over time: Gradually increase your contributions as your income grows or as you pay off other debts.

Windfalls: Dedicate a portion of bonuses, tax refunds, or side income directly to your emergency fund to accelerate growth.

Example: Saving $100 per week adds up to $5,200 a year, plus interest. This builds momentum and can grow faster when supplemented with larger one-off contributions.

6. Utilize Windfalls and Unexpected Income

Why It Matters: Unexpected income like bonuses, tax refunds, or inheritance can significantly boost your emergency fund. These are opportunities to make large contributions without disrupting your budget.

How to Do It:

Commit to saving 50-100% of any windfall directly into your emergency fund.

If you're saving for multiple goals (like retirement or a home), allocate a percentage to each, with a priority on the emergency fund.

Example: If you receive a $5,000 tax refund, save at least half ($2,500) into your emergency fund, and use the rest for other financial goals.

7. Adjust for Inflation and Lifestyle Changes

Why It Matters: Inflation and changes in your family size, living situation, or expenses can impact the amount you need in your emergency fund.

How to Do It:

Reevaluate your emergency fund goal yearly: Adjust your savings target to account for rising costs or changes in family dynamics (e.g., having children or a spouse).

If your expenses have increased by 5%, make sure to increase your fund by 5% as well.

Example: If inflation or lifestyle changes increase your monthly expenses from $3,000 to $3,500, increase your emergency fund target accordingly.

8. Keep the Fund Liquid but Protected

Why It Matters: An emergency fund should be easily accessible in times of need, but not so liquid that you're tempted to dip into it for non-emergencies.

How to Do It:

Keep your emergency fund in a high-yield savings account or money market account. Both offer liquidity and better returns than a traditional savings account.

Avoid investing emergency fund money in stocks or other volatile assets that could lose value during a market downturn.

Key Tip: Ensure that your fund is FDIC-insured, meaning it is protected up to $250,000 in case of bank failure.

9. Establish Clear Rules for Emergency Use

Why It Matters: Having clear guidelines for when to use your emergency fund helps you preserve it for true emergencies.

How to Do It:

Use the fund only for unplanned, essential expenses, like medical emergencies, job loss, or necessary home repairs.

Do not use it for discretionary expenses, vacations, or planned purchases.

If you do need to dip into your fund, make it a priority to replenish it as soon as possible.

Key Tip: Treat your emergency fund as insurance—it's there when you need it, but should remain untouched until a true emergency arises.

10. Replenish After Using the Fund

Why It Matters: If you ever need to dip into your emergency fund, it's crucial to replenish it quickly to ensure you remain financially secure for future emergencies.

How to Do It:

After using your emergency fund, temporarily increase your monthly savings contributions until you've restored it to its original level.

Avoid adding non-essential expenses back into your budget until your fund is fully replenished.

Example: If you use $2,000 of your emergency fund for car repairs, prioritize putting an extra $100-200 per month into the fund until it's restored.

Conclusion

A long-term emergency fund is your financial safety net, protecting you and your family from unexpected financial hardships. By setting a clear savings goal, budgeting effectively, using a high-yield savings account, and building consistent savings habits, you can create a strong, liquid emergency fund. This fund will ensure financial security and peace of mind, allowing you to navigate emergencies without resorting to debt or depleting long-term investments.

Quiz

How could unexpected emergencies like job loss or major car repairs, similar to Sarah's experience, drastically impact your financial situation, and how can an emergency fund protect you from falling into debt during such times?

____

____

What are some other severe emergencies—such as medical expenses or home repairs—that could lead to financial setbacks, and how does having an emergency fund help you handle these crises without relying on credit?

____

____

How much should you aim to save in an emergency fund to ensure you're adequately prepared for unexpected situations, and what strategies can you use to build this safety net over time?

____

____

Insurance

Clara, a 35-year-old school teacher, had always been a cautious person, especially when it came to finances. While she was good at saving and budgeting, one area overwhelmed her: insurance. Over the years, Clara had heard countless warnings from friends, family, and even financial advisors about the importance of being covered. Out of fear of being underinsured, she kept buying policies.

Whenever a new insurance agent approached her—whether it was at work, during a phone call, or through an ad—Clara felt pressured to purchase. She bought life insurance, disability insurance, critical illness policies, long-term care, and more. The problem was, Clara never fully understood what she was buying. Each time she signed up for a new policy, she told herself, "Better safe than sorry." By the time she turned 48, Clara had 22 insurance policies, but she had no idea how they worked or what they covered.

One day, Clara sat down to do a PFC (Personal Financial Check Up) with a Financial Professional and afterwards she organized her financial documents and realized the magnitude of her situation. She saw multiple policies with overlapping coverage—some were duplicates of others, and a few were costing her more than she could afford. Despite paying thousands of dollars annually in premiums, she wasn't even sure if she had the right protection for her needs.

Feeling frustrated and overwhelmed, Clara was helped by a financial professional. After reviewing all 22 policies, the professional explained that many of them were redundant, offering similar or identical coverage. Worse yet, Clara had been paying for some policies that didn't align with her goals or circumstances.

The Professional helped her simplify her insurance portfolio, canceling unnecessary or duplicate policies and consolidating the ones that were beneficial. They also took the time to educate Clara on how each policy worked and why it was or wasn't needed.

Clara felt a huge sense of relief. For the first time, she understood her coverage and could make informed decisions. She realized that insurance was important, but it needed to be part of a thoughtful plan—not something driven by fear.

From then on, Clara was much more confident in her financial decisions. She learned that it's not about having more policies—it's about having the right ones that fit your needs and future goals.

Using an Indexed Universal Life (IUL) insurance policy as part of someone's personal financial portfolio can provide a powerful combination of life insurance protection, tax advantages, and long-term wealth-building potential. Below is a comprehensive strategy on how to use an IUL policy as a financial tool, focusing on growth, protection, and leveraging the unique features of the policy for personal financial goals.

1. **Understand the Basics of IUL**

What Is IUL?

An Indexed Universal Life (IUL) policy is a type of permanent life insurance that provides a death benefit along with a cash value component. The cash value grows based on the performance of a market index, such as the S&P 500, but without the risk of losing money due to market declines.

Key Features:

Market-Linked Growth: The cash value grows based on a market index, with the opportunity for higher returns than traditional whole life policies.

Downside Protection: Typically, there's a guaranteed minimum interest rate (e.g., 0.25% floor), ensuring that even in market downturns, your cash value doesn't lose money.

Tax-Advantaged Growth: The growth of the cash value is tax-deferred, and loans or withdrawals from the policy can be tax-free if structured correctly.

Living Benefits: In the event the insured comes down with an illness or injury that results in a chronic, critical illness or terminal illness, the insured can access the death benefit early to pay for long-term care expenses and pay for other living expenses.

2. Leverage IUL for Tax-Free Retirement Income

Why It Works: IUL policies allow for tax-free withdrawals and policy loans against the accumulated cash value, which can be a valuable source of retirement income.

How to Do It:

Fund the Policy Early: Contribute to your IUL policy consistently and early in life to allow the cash value to grow substantially over time. Maximize contributions without exceeding Modified Endowment Contract (MEC) limits to preserve tax advantages.

Withdraw or Take Loans in Retirement: Once the policy has built up a significant cash value, you can take loans or withdrawals against the policy. These loans are typically tax-free and do not have to be repaid during your lifetime (they are repaid from the death benefit).

Example: If you accumulate $500,000 in cash value by retirement, you could take out $20,000-$30,000 per year tax-free for supplemental income, while the rest of the cash value continues to grow.

3. Use the IUL as a Safe Investment with Downside Protection

Why It Works: IUL policies provide growth potential linked to the stock market (via indexes like the S&P 500) while protecting your cash value from losses in down markets, thanks to a 0% floor.

How to Do It:

Index Allocation: Allocate your policy's cash value to different index accounts offered by the insurer. These accounts track market performance but offer a guaranteed floor, typically 0-2%, ensuring that you don't lose money in a market crash.

Diversify Growth Options: Some policies offer multiple indexing strategies with caps (e.g., capped at 12% gains). Diversify your index selections to balance growth potential with safety.

Example: In a year where the S&P 500 grows by 10%, your IUL cash value could reflect a 10% gain (subject to caps). In a year where the market drops by 20%, your policy's cash value might be credited with 0%, preserving your balance.

4. Use IUL for Estate Planning and Wealth Transfer

Why It Works: The death benefit of an IUL policy is typically tax-free to beneficiaries and can be used to transfer wealth efficiently.

How to Do It:

Set Up Beneficiaries: Designate family members or a trust as beneficiaries to ensure the tax-free death benefit passes to them upon your death.

Leave a Legacy: The death benefit can serve as a legacy tool, ensuring your family is financially protected. It can also be used to pay estate taxes or provide liquidity to settle the estate.

Use Living Benefits: Some IUL policies offer living benefits, such as the ability to access a portion of the death benefit early in cases of terminal illness or chronic care needs.

Example: If your IUL policy has a $1 million death benefit, your beneficiaries receive this amount tax-free, which could pay off debts, provide financial security, or cover estate taxes.

5. Take Advantage of IUL for College Funding

Why It Works: The cash value of an IUL can be used as a tax-free source of funds for college expenses without negatively affecting financial aid calculations (since it's not considered an asset in FAFSA).

How to Do It:

Build Cash Value During Your Child's Early Years: Begin funding the policy when your child is young, so the cash value has time to accumulate.

Withdraw or Take Loans for College: When your child reaches college age, you can take tax-free policy loans or withdrawals to cover tuition and expenses. This avoids student loan debt while maintaining financial aid eligibility.

Example: By contributing to an IUL starting when your child is born, you could accumulate a substantial amount (e.g., $50,000-$100,000) by the time they're 18, which can be used for college tuition without affecting financial aid.

6. Protect Your Wealth and Use IUL for Long-Term Care (LTC)

Why It Works: Many IUL policies offer optional long-term care (LTC) riders, which allow you to access the death benefit early to pay for long-term care expenses. This protects your retirement assets from being drained by healthcare costs.

How to Do It:

Add an LTC Rider: When purchasing your IUL policy, add an LTC rider. This ensures that if you need long-term care in the future, you can use a portion of your death benefit to cover those costs.

Use LTC Benefits: If you develop a chronic illness or disability requiring long-term care, you can access the policy's death benefit early without paying taxes on the amount used for care.

Example: If your IUL policy has a $500,000 death benefit and you need long-term care, you could access up to 50% ($250,000) of the death benefit to cover care costs, ensuring your other retirement assets remain intact.

7. Use IUL for Business and Key-Person Insurance

Why It Works: Business owners can use IUL policies to insure key employees or partners, ensuring financial stability for the business in the event of their death. The cash value can also be used for business expansion or to buy out a partner.

How to Do It:

Key-Person Insurance: Purchase IUL policies for key employees or partners. The business owns the policy and is the beneficiary, receiving the death benefit to cover financial losses or fund a replacement search if the insured dies.

Buy-Sell Agreements: Use an IUL policy as part of a buy-sell agreement, ensuring that in the event of a partner's death, the business can use the death benefit to buy out the deceased partner's share.

Cash Value for Business Expansion: After the policy has built significant cash value, the business can take policy loans to fund expansion or cover business expenses.

Example: A business with two partners each purchases an IUL policy on the other. If one partner dies, the death benefit allows the surviving partner to buy out the deceased partner's family and maintain control of the business.

8. Use IUL for Tax Diversification in Retirement

Why It Works: An IUL policy provides tax-free income in retirement, which can complement taxable retirement accounts like 401(k)s or IRAs. This tax diversification helps manage tax brackets and withdrawal strategies in retirement.

How to Do It:

Contribute to an IUL alongside 401(k) or IRA: Maximize contributions to tax-advantaged accounts like your 401(k) or IRA, but also fund an IUL policy. In retirement, you can withdraw from the IUL tax-free, minimizing taxable income from your 401(k) or IRA.

Strategize Withdrawals: Withdraw from taxable accounts up to certain tax thresholds, and supplement with tax-free loans from the IUL to reduce tax burdens.

Example: If your taxable income from 401(k) pushes you into a higher tax bracket, you can withdraw funds from your IUL policy instead, lowering your overall tax liability.

Conclusion

An IUL policy can be a highly versatile financial tool within a personal financial portfolio. It offers a combination of life insurance protection, tax-free income potential, and the ability to grow wealth through market-linked gains while protecting against market losses. Whether you're looking to build retirement income, fund college tuition, cover long-term care costs, or transfer wealth to your heirs, an IUL policy can serve multiple roles in your overall financial strategy.

Quiz

How does a term life insurance policy differ from whole life insurance in terms of duration and premium costs, and why might someone choose one over the other based on their financial goals?

____

____

What are the key benefits of a whole life insurance policy, such as the guaranteed cash value growth, compared to the flexible premium structure and growth potential offered by an Indexed Universal Life (IUL) policy?

____

____

How does an Indexed Universal Life (IUL) policy allow for cash value accumulation based on market index performance, and how does this differ from the fixed cash value growth in a whole life policy and the lack of cash value in term life insurance?

____

____

To maximize the benefits of an IUL, work with a financial professional

(Larry Winters phone 661-440-1711 email: agentlarryw@yahoo.com)

to ensure the policy is structured correctly and aligns with your personal financial goals.

Real Estate

Terry had always been cautious with her money, growing up in a family that valued financial security. She worked hard at her job as an accountant, saved diligently, and lived comfortably. But deep down, she always wanted something more—a way to build wealth that wasn't just tied to her paycheck.

One day, after hearing her friend talk about how investing in real estate had changed his life, Terry began to seriously consider buying property. The idea of owning real estate scared her at first—she'd heard horror stories of bad tenants, market crashes, and expensive repairs. But after months of research and talking to a trusted real estate agent, Terry decided to take the plunge.

At 62, Terry bought her first rental property, a small duplex in a growing neighborhood. She used her savings for the down payment and secured a manageable mortgage. After screening for reliable tenants, she found renters for both units almost immediately.

The steady monthly rental income quickly covered her mortgage payments, and within a year, Terry realized she was earning extra income she hadn't anticipated. Not only was she paying down her mortgage, but she also had cash flow that allowed her to invest in property maintenance, upgrades, and even another rental property a few years later.

As time passed, Terry's properties increased in value. She watched as the real estate market in her city grew, and with it, her wealth. Not only was she building equity in her homes, but the passive income allowed her to take financial risks she never thought possible—like investing in other ventures, funding her children's education, and even taking vacations she had once deemed too expensive.

Terry looked back on her decision to become a property owner with pride. What started as a scary leap of faith had turned into one of the best decisions of her life. Real estate had not only provided her with financial security but also with opportunities she wouldn't have had otherwise. Her properties were now a source of passive income that would support her well into her retirement.

Owning real estate gave Terry more than just financial gain—it gave her peace of mind and freedom. She realized that sometimes, the best investments are the ones that take you out of your comfort zone, but with proper research and patience, they can lead to life-changing rewards.

When deciding to start building a real estate portfolio, it can be one of the most effective ways to generate long-term wealth, passive income, and financial security. A well-planned strategy allows for scaling up from a single property to multiple income-generating properties while managing risks and optimizing returns. Here's the best step-by-step strategy for building a successful real estate portfolio.

1. Establish Clear Financial Goals

Why It's Important: Your goals will determine the types of properties you invest in, your budget, and your risk tolerance. Establishing clear objectives helps keep your strategy focused and aligned with your long-term financial vision.

How to Do It:

Decide on short-term vs. long-term goals: Do you want passive income, long-term appreciation, or both?

Set a target for how many properties or how much income you want to generate within a specific timeframe (e.g., own 5 properties in 5 years, or generate $10,000/month in passive income).

Evaluate your risk tolerance and time horizon (flipping vs. holding properties for decades).

Example: A goal could be to retire in 10 years by building a real estate portfolio that generates $5,000 in monthly cash flow from rental income.

2. Build Your Financial Foundation

Why It's Important: Lenders will review your financial health, including your credit score, debt-to-income (DTI) ratio, and liquid assets, before approving loans. Strong finances ensure better loan terms and faster portfolio growth.

How to Do It:

Improve Your Credit Score: Aim for a score above 700 to secure favorable mortgage rates.

Reduce Debt: Pay down high-interest debts to improve your DTI ratio.

Save for Down Payments: For investment properties, plan to put down 20%-25% of the property's value to avoid private mortgage insurance (PMI).

Create an Emergency Fund: Set aside 6-12 months of living and property expenses for contingencies.

Example: By reducing debt and saving $50,000, you'll be in a strong financial position to make down payments on multiple properties with better loan terms.

3. Start with One Property and Learn the Ropes

Why It's Important: Starting with one property allows you to learn property management, deal with tenants, and understand cash flow mechanics. Gaining experience on a small scale helps avoid costly mistakes when scaling up.

How to Do It:

Buy a Single-Family Home or Duplex: Start with a property type that's relatively easy to manage and affordable.

House Hacking: Buy a duplex or triplex, live in one unit, and rent out the others. This allows you to leverage owner-occupied financing options, which typically require a lower down payment.

Learn the Numbers: Calculate your cash flow, net operating income (NOI), and return on investment (ROI). Make sure the property is cash-flow positive after accounting for mortgage, taxes, insurance, and maintenance.

Example: Purchase a duplex for $200,000, live in one unit, and rent out the other for $1,000/month. If your mortgage and expenses total $1,500/month, you're living for $500/month while building equity.

4. Leverage Financing and Expand with Equity

Why It's Important: Leveraging financing (using other people's money) allows you to scale your portfolio faster. As your first property appreciates, you can use the equity to acquire additional properties.

How to Do It:

Refinance or Use HELOC: After your first property appreciates or you build enough equity, refinance or take a home equity line of credit (HELOC) to pull out the equity for a down payment on another property.

Use Conventional Loans: Conventional loans with 20%-25% down can be used to finance multiple investment properties, especially if your DTI ratio is strong.

Consider Seller Financing or Partnerships: In competitive markets, explore creative financing options like seller financing, where the seller holds the mortgage, or form partnerships with other investors to pool resources.

Example: If your first property appreciates from $200,000 to $250,000, you can refinance and pull out $40,000 in equity to fund the purchase of your next property.

5. Diversify Property Types and Locations

Why It's Important: Diversification reduces risk and improves stability. If one market or property type underperforms, other properties in different locations or asset classes may perform better.

How to Do It:

Types of Properties: Consider diversifying into single-family homes, multi-family properties (duplexes, triplexes), vacation rentals, or commercial properties (office spaces, retail).

Geographic Diversification: Invest in different cities or states where real estate markets are growing. Avoid concentrating all your properties in one area to mitigate risk from local market downturns or economic changes.

Different Strategies: Diversify your investment strategy by combining long-term buy-and-hold rentals with shorter-term flips, vacation rentals, or commercial leases.

Example: If you own two single-family homes, consider purchasing a small apartment complex in a different city or invest in a short-term vacation rental in a high-tourism area to diversify your portfolio.

6. Scale Smartly with the BRRRR Method

Why It's Important: The BRRRR Method (Buy, Rehab, Rent, Refinance, Repeat) is an excellent strategy for scaling your portfolio quickly by recycling capital.

How to Do It:

Buy: Purchase an undervalued property that needs cosmetic or structural repairs.

Rehab: Renovate the property to increase its value.

Rent: Rent out the property for consistent cash flow.

Refinance: Once the property's value increases after renovation, refinance to pull out the equity.

Repeat: Use the refinanced capital to buy your next investment property and repeat the process.

Example: Buy a fixer-upper for $150,000, invest $30,000 in renovations, and increase its value to $220,000. Refinance to pull out $50,000 of equity and purchase your next property.

7. Optimize Cash Flow and Property Management

Why It's Important: Positive cash flow is crucial for portfolio sustainability and growth. Effective property management ensures profitability, minimizes vacancies, and reduces tenant issues.

How to Do It:

Analyze Properties for Cash Flow: Use tools like cash-on-cash return and NOI to evaluate potential purchases. Look for properties that generate 8%-12% annual returns.

Use Professional Property Management: As you scale, managing multiple properties can be time-consuming. Hiring a property management company (typically for 8%-10% of monthly rent) can handle tenant screening, rent collection, and maintenance, allowing you to focus on growth.

Reduce Vacancies: Minimize turnover by keeping rental rates competitive, maintaining the property well, and fostering good tenant relationships.

Example: For a rental property generating $2,000/month in rent, after mortgage, taxes, insurance, and management fees, ensure the net cash flow is positive (e.g., $400/month) and invest that surplus into property improvements or new purchases.

8. Use Tax Strategies to Your Advantage

Why It's Important: Real estate offers numerous tax benefits that can significantly increase your returns. Taking advantage of tax deductions and strategies helps you keep more profits.

How to Do It:

Depreciation: Real estate investors can depreciate the value of the property over time (27.5 years for residential properties), reducing taxable income.

Tax Deductions: Deduct property expenses, mortgage interest, property management fees, maintenance costs, and more.

1031 Exchange: Use a 1031 exchange to defer capital gains taxes when selling one investment property and reinvesting the proceeds into another.

Opportunity Zones: Invest in opportunity zones to receive tax incentives for capital gains.

Example: If you earn $20,000 in rental income from a property, use deductions and depreciation to reduce taxable income to $10,000, saving on taxes and reinvesting the difference into growing your portfolio.

9. Continuously Reinvest Profits and Scale

Why It's Important: Reinvesting your rental income and appreciation profits allows you to accelerate your portfolio growth. Compound your wealth by strategically using the cash flow from your existing properties to fund new investments.

How to Do It:

Use Cash Flow for Down Payments: Instead of spending rental income, save and reinvest it as down payments for future properties.

Sell and Upgrade Properties: As the market appreciates, sell underperforming properties and use the proceeds to buy higher-quality or larger properties.

Portfolio Reviews: Regularly review your portfolio for underperforming assets, and make adjustments such as selling or refinancing.

Example: Reinvest $10,000 in annual cash flow into your next property purchase, which then generates an additional $500/month in rental income, creating a snowball effect that allows you to expand faster.

10. Plan for Long-Term Wealth and Exit Strategy

Why It's Important: Planning how you will exit your investments ensures you maximize returns and preserve wealth for retirement or your heirs.

How to Do It:

Sell or Hold for Cash Flow: Decide whether to hold properties for passive income in retirement or sell them to fund other ventures. Consider keeping properties with strong cash flow or appreciation potential.

Set Up an Estate Plan: Ensure your properties are structured to minimize taxes upon inheritance and that they are passed on efficiently to your heirs through proper estate planning.

Prepare for Market Downturns: Keep a cash reserve and adjust your portfolio to weather market fluctuations. During downturns, consider holding properties instead of selling at a loss.

Example: After building a portfolio of 10 properties, you decide to sell 5 and keep the others for passive income in retirement, generating $7,000 per month in cash flow.

Quiz

How can owning real estate, like Terry did, help you build equity over time, and why is this accumulation of property value a key factor in creating generational wealth?

____

____

What role does rental income from investment properties play in providing long-term, passive income that can be passed down to future generations, and how does this income stream contribute to family financial security?

____

____

How does real estate appreciation and the ability to leverage property through refinancing or selling enable families to grow wealth across generations, and what advantages does real estate offer compared to other investment options for long-term wealth building?

____

____

Bonus Material

Here's a general timeline and overview of the history of gentrification, along with its driving forces.

Late 19th Century to Early 20th Century: Urbanization and Industrialization

Context: In the late 1800s, the process of rapid urbanization began due to industrialization, especially in cities in the U.S., the UK, and Europe. As cities expanded, wealthier individuals moved away from the crowded inner cities to more affluent suburban areas, leaving behind urban cores populated by the working class and marginalized communities.

Purpose: The movement out of the inner cities was driven by a desire for more space and the emerging ideal of suburban living. There was no intentional push to displace residents, but this era set the stage for the spatial divides that would later be relevant in gentrification.

1950s: Suburbanization and White Flight

Context: After World War II, government policies such as the G.I. Bill and subsidized loans fueled the growth of suburbs in the United States. Many middle- and upper-class families (predominantly white) moved to suburban neighborhoods, leaving city centers increasingly populated by low-income, minority groups. The decline in urban populations led to disinvestment in inner-city areas.

Purpose: Suburbanization was part of broader socio-political shifts in post-war development, often driven by government policies favoring suburban expansion and home ownership.

1960s: Gentrification as a Concept Emerges

1964: British sociologist Ruth Glass coins the term "gentrification" while describing the transformation of working-class neighborhoods in London, where more affluent middle-class residents began moving into traditionally lower-income areas.

Purpose: Gentrification, as observed by Glass, was the process by which wealthier individuals move into lower-income neighborhoods, renovating properties, and increasing property values, thus displacing lower-income residents.

1970s–1980s: Gentrification Expands in the U.S.

Context: Gentrification becomes more noticeable in major U.S. cities such as New York, San Francisco, and Boston. Urban renewal projects initiated by governments, often backed by private developers, begin to transform deteriorating neighborhoods. In cities like New York, artists and middle-class professionals start moving into areas like SoHo and Tribeca, renovating lofts and warehouses.

Purpose: The economic incentives were key drivers, as cities sought to revitalize decaying downtown areas and attract a wealthier tax base. Cultural shifts also played a role, as urban living became more desirable, especially for professionals.

1990s: Urban Renewal and the "Back-to-the-City" Movement

Context: The 1990s saw a continued revival of interest in urban living. With crime rates declining and cities investing in infrastructure, young professionals and "empty-nesters" started returning to cities. Many neighborhoods were transformed by new development, often at the expense of existing lower-income residents who could no longer afford rising rents.

Purpose: Local governments, developers, and city planners aimed to attract a higher-income population to cities to stimulate economic growth, increase property values, and improve urban amenities.

2000s–2010s: Widespread Gentrification and Global Trends

Context: Gentrification became a widespread phenomenon, not only in large cities like New York and San Francisco but also in smaller cities and globally (e.g., in cities like London, Paris, and Berlin). Technology hubs (e.g., Silicon Valley, Brooklyn) became magnets for gentrification, where wealth from tech companies drove up housing prices.

Purpose: The purpose behind gentrification now included attracting tech workers, improving city infrastructure, and creating new cultural spaces, such as restaurants, cafes, and boutiques. In many cases, the goal was to make cities more competitive on a global scale.

2020s: Gentrification and Social Equity Concerns

Context: Gentrification remains a contentious issue, especially with rising income inequality and housing shortages in major cities. The effects on minority communities, affordable housing, and cultural displacement have sparked debates around policy changes to manage or slow gentrification. Calls for affordable housing, rent control, and anti-displacement measures have grown louder.

Purpose: Governments and developers still see gentrification as a tool for economic development, but there is increasing pressure to balance these goals with equity and inclusion to prevent the displacement of long-time residents.

Driving Forces Behind Gentrification:

Economic Opportunity: Cities and developers seek to increase property values, attract investment, and improve the tax base.

Urban Renewal: Governments and planners promote the redevelopment of decayed areas to revitalize cities.

Cultural Shifts: A growing preference for urban living, especially among younger generations, professionals, and creatives.

Social Displacement: As wealthier residents move in, property values rise, leading to the displacement of lower-income residents due to higher rents and property taxes.

Globalization: Global cities compete for talent and investment, often encouraging gentrification as a way to present themselves as modern and attractive to international elites.

Conclusion

Gentrification is a complex process that has evolved over time, from the suburbanization of the 1950s to the current concerns over displacement and equity. While it has brought economic development and urban revitalization, it has also raised issues of social justice, particularly in the displacement of marginalized communities.

History of the Realtist Movement and the National Association of Real Estate Brokers (NAREB)

The term "Realtist" refers to members of the National Association of Real Estate Brokers (NAREB), an organization founded to represent the interests of African American and minority real estate professionals and communities. The story of how the Realtist movement came about is rooted in the history of racial segregation and discrimination in the real estate industry.

1947: Formation of the National Association of Real Estate Brokers (NAREB)

Context: During the first half of the 20th century, African Americans faced significant racial discrimination in housing and real estate. Black real estate professionals were systematically excluded from mainstream organizations like the National Association of Realtors (NAR) due to segregationist policies, and African American homebuyers were often restricted from purchasing homes in certain areas because of practices like redlining and racial covenants.

Purpose: In response to these exclusionary practices, 12 African American real estate professionals founded the National Association of Real Estate Brokers (NAREB) on July 29, 1947, in Tampa, Florida. NAREB's primary goal was to promote fair housing and provide a platform for African American real estate professionals to work within an organization that supported their professional development, networking, and the ability to represent minority communities.

NAREB's Core Mission and Advocacy

Fair Housing and Equal Opportunity: From its inception, NAREB advocated for fair housing practices and the elimination of discriminatory practices in real estate, such as redlining (the practice of denying services, typically financial, to residents of certain areas based on their race or ethnicity).

Professional Empowerment: The association sought to provide African Americans with the training, certification, and networking opportunities they were denied elsewhere, allowing them to excel as real estate professionals.

Community Development: NAREB has always been deeply rooted in the empowerment of African American communities, advocating for homeownership as a means to build wealth and improve living standards. Their slogan, "Democracy in Housing," reflects this mission to ensure that homeownership and property investment opportunities are available to all, regardless of race.

Difference Between a Realtist and a Real Estate Agent

Realtist:

A Realtist is a member of the National Association of Real Estate Brokers (NAREB), which focuses on promoting "Democracy in Housing" and advocating for equal housing opportunities, particularly for African Americans and other minority communities.

Realtists work to eliminate discriminatory practices in the housing market and provide a space for Black real estate professionals, given the historical exclusion from other associations like the National Association of Realtors (NAR).

Realtists are deeply involved in advocating for minority homeownership, ensuring fair housing policies, and fighting against housing discrimination.

Real Estate Agent:

A Real Estate Agent is a professional who is licensed to assist buyers and sellers in real estate transactions. They typically help clients buy, sell, or rent properties, and their primary function is to facilitate transactions.

Real estate agents can become Realtors, which means they are members of the National Association of Realtors (NAR), the largest trade association for real estate professionals in the U.S.

Realtors must adhere to the NAR Code of Ethics, a set of guidelines that emphasizes professionalism, fairness, and integrity in dealing with clients and the public. However, unlike NAREB, NAR was historically less focused on fair housing advocacy for minority communities.

Key Differences:

Membership Organizations:

Realtist: Member of NAREB, which focuses on minority communities and advocates for fair housing.

Realtor: Member of NAR, the mainstream organization for real estate professionals, with a focus on ethical standards for real estate transactions.

Mission and Focus:

Realtist: Dedicated to fighting housing discrimination, promoting minority homeownership, and ensuring equal access to real estate opportunities.

Real Estate Agent/Realtor: Primarily focused on facilitating real estate transactions and adhering to ethical standards.

Historical Context:

Realtist: Born out of a need for an organization that represented African American real estate professionals who were excluded from NAR due to segregation.

Realtor: Part of the broader, historically dominant organization in real estate, which did not initially prioritize minority inclusion.

Conclusion:

While both Realtists and Realtors work in real estate, the key difference lies in their professional organizations and the focus of their advocacy. Realtists, as members of NAREB, have a long history of advocating for civil rights and fair housing, with a special emphasis on serving the African American community. Realtors, members of NAR, are part of the largest and most mainstream organization in the industry, which also supports ethical real estate practices, but without the same civil rights-focused mission that defines the Realtist movement.

"A good man leaves an inheritance to his children's children, but the sinner's wealth is laid up for the righteous" Locations Proverbs 13:22

Business Owner

Not everyone is cut out to become a successful business owner. Some may be okay with living a mediocre life. But in order to become a successful business owner, it involves careful planning, strategic execution, and a continuous commitment to growth. Below is a detailed strategy for building, launching, and sustaining a business from the ground up.

1. Identify Your Niche and Business Idea

Why It's Important: A strong, clear business idea that fills a market gap or solves a problem is the foundation of any successful business. Finding a niche helps you stand out and attract a targeted audience.

How to Do It:

Assess Your Skills and Passions: Start with what you're good at and passionate about. These areas often lead to business ideas where you can add the most value.

Market Research: Identify market trends, consumer needs, and gaps in the current market. Research competitors and see where there are opportunities for innovation or improved customer service.

Validate Your Idea: Test your business idea by gathering feedback from potential customers or running small-scale tests before fully launching.

Example: If you're passionate about fitness and see a gap in affordable personal training for beginners, you can focus on creating a business that provides personalized fitness coaching at a lower price point than current market options.

2. Write a Comprehensive Business Plan

Why It's Important: A business plan serves as a roadmap, outlining your strategy for growth, funding, marketing, and operations. It helps clarify your vision and allows you to pitch your business to investors or lenders.

How to Do It:

Executive Summary: Briefly describe your business, its mission, target market, and the problem it solves.

Market Research: Include detailed information on your target market, competitor analysis, and industry trends.

Financial Plan: Outline your budget, projected expenses, pricing strategy, and revenue forecasts. Include a break-even analysis and funding requirements.

Marketing and Sales Strategy: Define how you will attract and retain customers. Outline advertising methods, customer acquisition costs, and sales processes.

Operational Plan: Detail the logistics of running the business, such as staffing, supply chains, technology, and day-to-day operations.

Example: If you're starting an online boutique, your business plan would include an analysis of e-commerce trends, target demographics (e.g., women ages 18-35), and how you'll use social media marketing to drive sales.

3. Secure Funding and Financial Resources

Why It's Important: Having sufficient capital is critical for launching, growing, and sustaining a business. Funding can cover startup costs, operations, marketing, and expansion.

How to Do It:

Bootstrapping: Start with your personal savings, especially if you have a low-cost business model. This gives you full ownership and control.

Small Business Loans: Consider applying for small business loans from banks, credit unions, or government-backed programs (like the U.S. Small Business Administration).

Angel Investors or Venture Capital: For high-growth potential businesses, seek investment from angel investors or venture capital firms in exchange for equity.

Crowdfunding: Platforms like Kickstarter or Indiegogo allow you to raise money directly from supporters and future customers.

Grants: Research and apply for small business grants, particularly those targeting underrepresented groups, industries, or innovation.

Example: If you're starting a tech startup, you could secure $100,000 in seed funding from angel investors to cover development costs and initial marketing.

4. Choose the Right Business Structure

Why It's Important: Your business structure affects everything from day-to-day operations to personal liability, taxes, and the ability to raise money.

How to Do It:

Sole Proprietorship: The simplest form, with no separation between you and the business. Ideal for freelancers and small side businesses but carries unlimited liability.

Limited Liability Company (LLC): Provides limited liability protection while offering flexibility in taxation. One of the most popular structures for small business owners.

Corporation (C-Corp or S-Corp): A more complex structure with formal regulations but offers the ability to raise capital through shares. C-Corps are taxed separately from their owners, while S-Corps allow profits to pass through to owners' personal tax returns.

Partnership: Two or more individuals share ownership, profits, and responsibilities. Suitable for businesses with multiple founders.

Example: If you're launching a consulting firm with one partner, an LLC would provide liability protection for both of you, while allowing profits to pass through to your personal taxes.

5. Register Your Business and Legal Setup

Why It's Important: Legal registration ensures your business is recognized by the government, protects your brand, and ensures compliance with laws.

How to Do It:

Register Your Business Name: Choose a unique name for your business and register it with the appropriate state or national agency.

Obtain Licenses and Permits: Research the necessary licenses and permits for your industry, such as health permits, zoning licenses, or professional certifications.

Get a Tax ID Number: Apply for an Employer Identification Number (EIN) from the IRS to use for tax purposes.

Set Up a Business Bank Account: Separate your personal and business finances by opening a business bank account. This simplifies accounting and protects personal assets.

Example: If you're opening a coffee shop, you'll need a food service license, business registration with your state, and a local health inspection certificate before you open.

6. Develop a Strong Brand Identity

Why It's Important: Your brand defines how customers perceive your business. A consistent, strong brand identity builds trust and differentiates you from competitors.

How to Do It:

Create a Logo and Visual Identity: Design a professional logo and choose brand colors, fonts, and imagery that reflect your business values and target audience.

Develop Your Brand Voice: Define how you'll communicate with customers. Will your brand be professional and authoritative, fun and casual, or innovative and tech-savvy?

Build a Website: Your website serves as a digital storefront. Make it professional, easy to navigate, and optimized for SEO.

Use Social Media: Leverage platforms like Instagram, Facebook, LinkedIn, or TikTok to grow your audience, engage with customers, and promote your business.

Example: For an eco-friendly clothing line, you could create a brand around sustainability with earthy colors, a minimalist logo, and messaging focused on environmental responsibility.

7. Launch a Marketing and Sales Strategy

Why It's Important: Effective marketing drives customers to your business, while a solid sales strategy converts interest into revenue.

How to Do It:

Digital Marketing: Use social media, content marketing, email marketing, and paid ads to attract and engage your target audience.

SEO and Local Search: Optimize your website for search engines to ensure customers find you online. For local businesses, register with Google My Business to appear in local search results.

Networking and Partnerships: Attend industry events, join local business associations, and build relationships with potential clients, suppliers, and partners.

Referral Programs: Encourage satisfied customers to refer others by offering incentives like discounts or cash rewards for referrals.

Sales Funnel: Create a clear sales funnel that guides prospects from initial awareness to making a purchase. Follow up with leads and nurture relationships.

Example: An online marketing strategy for a yoga studio could include Instagram ads, blog posts about mindfulness, and email newsletters offering discounts on classes for new signups.

8. Hire a Strong Team

Why It's Important: A motivated, skilled team is essential to growing and scaling your business. As your business expands, you'll need the right people to manage operations, sales, marketing, and customer service.

How to Do It:

Determine Key Roles: Identify the positions critical to your business success (e.g., sales, operations, marketing, customer service).

Hire for Culture Fit: Look for employees who align with your company's values and are passionate about the business.

Outsource Where Needed: Consider outsourcing non-core tasks, such as accounting, IT, or marketing, to freelancers or agencies, especially if you can't afford full-time hires at first.

Train and Develop: Provide ongoing training and development opportunities for your team to improve their skills and loyalty.

Example: A tech startup might hire a small team of developers and salespeople, while outsourcing marketing to a digital marketing agency.

9. Monitor Your Finances and KPIs

Why It's Important: Keeping track of your finances ensures profitability, sustainability, and growth. Monitoring key performance indicators (KPIs) helps you make informed business decisions.

How to Do It:

Track Revenue and Expenses: Use accounting software like QuickBooks or Xero to monitor cash flow, manage invoices, and track expenses.

Monitor Profit Margins: Ensure that your profit margins are healthy by regularly reviewing your costs and pricing strategy.

Measure KPIs: Track KPIs such as customer acquisition cost (CAC), lifetime value (LTV), sales growth, and website traffic to assess your business's health.

Review Financial Statements: Regularly review income statements, balance sheets, and cash flow statements to understand your financial position. Example: A retail business might track KPIs like average transaction value, foot traffic, and return on marketing investment to ensure the store is performing well.

10. Scale Your Business

Why It's Important: Once your business is profitable and stable, scaling allows you to increase revenue and grow your market share.

How to Do It:

Expand Product or Service Lines: Introduce new products, services, or variations to appeal to a broader audience.

Open New Locations: For brick-and-mortar businesses, expanding to new areas can help increase customer reach and revenue.

Invest in Technology: Automate processes, improve customer experience, and reduce costs by investing in technology solutions, such as e-commerce platforms, CRM systems, or inventory management software.

Seek Strategic Partnerships: Partner with other businesses to reach new markets, share resources, or collaborate on product development.

Franchising: For some businesses, franchising can be a viable way to scale rapidly without taking on the full financial burden of expansion.

Example: A successful restaurant might expand by opening new locations in nearby cities or offering franchise opportunities to other entrepreneurs.

Conclusion

Becoming a business owner requires a combination of clear vision, effective planning, disciplined execution, and a willingness to adapt and grow. By focusing on a strong business foundation, securing adequate funding, and creating a sustainable growth strategy, you can build a business that thrives in the long term. Each step, from market research to scaling, plays a crucial role in ensuring the success of your entrepreneurial journey.

Quiz

How does owning a business allow individuals to create multiple income streams and increase their earning potential, making it a significant pathway to building wealth and financial independence?

____

____

In what ways does being a business owner provide opportunities for asset accumulation, such as property, inventory, and intellectual property, that contribute to long-term prosperity and financial security?

____

____

How does the ability to reinvest profits back into the business and take advantage of tax benefits create a favorable financial environment for business owners, positioning them for sustained growth and wealth generation?

____

____

Insurance

How can understanding different types of insurance policies help you make informed decisions about your financial security?

What are the key factors to consider when evaluating whether you have adequate insurance coverage for your needs?

How does having the right insurance policies in place protect your assets and provide peace of mind?

Real Estate

What are the long-term benefits of owning real estate compared to renting, especially regarding wealth accumulation?

How can real estate investments provide passive income streams, and what impact does this have on financial stability?

In what ways does property appreciation contribute to generational wealth, and how can you leverage it for future investments?

Taxes

What tax deductions and credits are available to you, and how can they significantly impact your overall financial situation?

How does strategic tax planning help you retain more of your earnings and increase your investment potential?

What are the potential consequences of not being aware of tax regulations, and how can proactive management prevent financial setbacks?

Investing

How does diversifying your investment portfolio mitigate risks and enhance potential returns?

____

____

What role does understanding market trends play in making informed investment decisions?

____

____

How can setting clear investment goals guide your strategy and ensure you remain focused on long-term growth?

____

____

Business Ownership

What are the key advantages of owning a business compared to being an employee in terms of wealth-building potential?

____

____

How does entrepreneurship provide opportunities for innovation and growth that can lead to financial prosperity?

____

____

In what ways can networking and building relationships in your industry enhance your business success and revenue?

____

____

Compound Interest

How does starting to invest early maximize the benefits of compound interest over time?

____

____

What are the common misconceptions about compound interest, and how can understanding its true nature change your savings strategy?

____

____

How can leveraging compound interest in different financial vehicles accelerate your path to financial independence?

____

____

Credit

What are the long-term benefits of maintaining a strong credit score, and how does it affect your ability to borrow and invest?

____

____

How can understanding credit utilization ratios help you improve your credit score over time?

____

____

In what ways can leveraging credit responsibly create opportunities for wealth-building through investments and business ownership?

____

____

Debt

What strategies can you implement to manage and reduce debt effectively, preventing it from hindering your financial progress?

____

____

How can understanding the difference between good debt and bad debt influence your borrowing decisions?

____

____

What role does a debt repayment plan, like the snowball or avalanche method, play in achieving financial freedom?

____

____

This term "Fiat" refers to a type of currency that a government declares to be legal tender, but it is not backed by a physical commodity like gold or silver. The value of fiat money is derived from the relationship between supply and demand and the stability of the issuing government, rather than an intrinsic value or material worth.

Key Characteristics of Fiat Currency:

Government-Issued: It is created and regulated by a central authority, typically a country's government or central bank.

Not Backed by Commodities: Unlike commodity money (e.g., gold or silver), fiat money is not linked to any physical asset. Its value comes from the trust and confidence people have in the government that issues it.

Inflation Risk: Since fiat money can be printed or removed from circulation at will, it is susceptible to inflation or even hyperinflation if too much money is printed.

Legal Tender: It must be accepted as a means of payment within the issuing country, as mandated by law.

Examples of Fiat Currencies:

The U.S. Dollar (USD)

The Euro (EUR)

The Japanese Yen (JPY)

The British Pound (GBP)

Please note that Fiat money is the most common form of currency in use today globally, facilitating everyday transactions, government policies, and international trade.

The Earlier you start
The Better!!

	Month				Year					
Expenses	**Day**	**Day**	**Day**	**Day**	**Day**	**Day**	**Day**	**Day**	**Day**	**Day**
Mortgage/ Rent	$	$	$	$	$	$	$	$	$	$
Electricity/ Gas	$	$	$	$	$	$	$	$	$	$
Water/trash	$	$	$	$	$	$	$	$	$	$
Internet/subscriptions	$	$	$	$	$	$	$	$	$	$
Auto insurance	$	$	$	$	$	$	$	$	$	$
Life insurance	$	$	$	$	$	$	$	$	$	$
Loans	$	$	$	$	$	$	$	$	$	$
Savings/ investment	$	$	$	$	$	$	$	$	$	$
Cell phone	$	$	$	$	$	$	$	$	$	$
Credit card	$	$	$	$	$	$	$	$	$	$
Transportation	$	$	$	$	$	$	$	$	$	$
Childcare	$	$	$	$	$	$	$	$	$	$
Groceries	$	$	$	$	$	$	$	$	$	$
Dining out	$	$	$	$	$	$	$	$	$	$
Clothing	$	$	$	$	$	$	$	$	$	$
Laundry/cleaning	$	$	$	$	$	$	$	$	$	$
Medical/prescriptions	$	$	$	$	$	$	$	$	$	$
Donations	$	$	$	$	$	$	$	$	$	$
Entertainment	$	$	$	$	$	$	$	$	$	$
Miscellaneous	$	$	$	$	$	$	$	$	$	$

Budget Sheets

Income 1		Income 2		Additional Income		First Week		Second Week		Third Week	
$	$	$	$	$	$	$	$	$	$	$	$
$	$	$	$	$	$	$	$	$	$	$	$
$	$	$	$	$	$	$	$	$	$	$	$
$	$	$	$	$	$	$	$	$	$	$	$
Totals											
$	$	$	$	$	$	$	$	$	$	$	$
				Total Income	$					**Total Income**	$
-Monthly Expenses											**-Monthly Expenses**
$										$	
Monthly Budget											**Monthly Budget**
$										$	
+Margin (left over)											**+Margin (left over)**
$										$	

	Month				Year					
Expenses	**Day**	**Day**	**Day**	**Day**	**Day**	**Day**	**Day**	**Day**	**Day**	**Day**
Mortgage/ Rent	$	$	$	$	$	$	$	$	$	$
Electricity/ Gas	$	$	$	$	$	$	$	$	$	$
Water/trash	$	$	$	$	$	$	$	$	$	$
Internet/subscriptions	$	$	$	$	$	$	$	$	$	$
Auto insurance	$	$	$	$	$	$	$	$	$	$
Life insurance	$	$	$	$	$	$	$	$	$	$
Loans	$	$	$	$	$	$	$	$	$	$
Savings/ investment	$	$	$	$	$	$	$	$	$	$
Cell phone	$	$	$	$	$	$	$	$	$	$
Credit card	$	$	$	$	$	$	$	$	$	$
Transportation	$	$	$	$	$	$	$	$	$	$
Childcare	$	$	$	$	$	$	$	$	$	$
Groceries	$	$	$	$	$	$	$	$	$	$
Dining out	$	$	$	$	$	$	$	$	$	$
Clothing	$	$	$	$	$	$	$	$	$	$
Laundry/cleaning	$	$	$	$	$	$	$	$	$	$
Medical/prescriptions	$	$	$	$	$	$	$	$	$	$
Donations	$	$	$	$	$	$	$	$	$	$
Entertainment	$	$	$	$	$	$	$	$	$	$
Miscellaneous	$	$	$	$	$	$	$	$	$	$

Income 1		**Income 2**		**Additional Income**		**First Week**		**Second Week**		**Third Week**	
$	$	$	$	$	$	$	$	$	$	$	$
$	$	$	$	$	$	$	$	$	$	$	$
$	$	$	$	$	$	$	$	$	$	$	$
$	$	$	$	$	$	$	$	$	$	$	$
Totals											
$	$	$	$	$	$	$	$	$	$	$	$
				Total Income	$					**Total Income**	$
-Monthly Expenses										**-Monthly Expenses**	
$										$	
Monthly Budget										**Monthly Budget**	
$										$	
+Margin (left over)										**+Margin (left over)**	
$										$	

	Month				Year					
Expenses	**Day**	**Day**	**Day**	**Day**	**Day**	**Day**	**Day**	**Day**	**Day**	**Day**
Mortgage/ Rent	$	$	$	$	$	$	$	$	$	$
Electricity/ Gas	$	$	$	$	$	$	$	$	$	$
Water/trash	$	$	$	$	$	$	$	$	$	$
Internet/subscriptions	$	$	$	$	$	$	$	$	$	$
Auto insurance	$	$	$	$	$	$	$	$	$	$
Life insurance	$	$	$	$	$	$	$	$	$	$
Loans	$	$	$	$	$	$	$	$	$	$
Savings/ investment	$	$	$	$	$	$	$	$	$	$
Cell phone	$	$	$	$	$	$	$	$	$	$
Credit card	$	$	$	$	$	$	$	$	$	$
Transportation	$	$	$	$	$	$	$	$	$	$
Childcare	$	$	$	$	$	$	$	$	$	$
Groceries	$	$	$	$	$	$	$	$	$	$
Dining out	$	$	$	$	$	$	$	$	$	$
Clothing	$	$	$	$	$	$	$	$	$	$
Laundry/cleaning	$	$	$	$	$	$	$	$	$	$
Medical/prescriptions	$	$	$	$	$	$	$	$	$	$
Donations	$	$	$	$	$	$	$	$	$	$
Entertainment	$	$	$	$	$	$	$	$	$	$
Miscellaneous	$	$	$	$	$	$	$	$	$	$

Income 1		**Income 2**		**Additional Income**		**First Week**		**Second Week**		**Third Week**	
$	$	$	$	$	$	$	$	$	$	$	$
$	$	$	$	$	$	$	$	$	$	$	$
$	$	$	$	$	$	$	$	$	$	$	$
$	$	$	$	$	$	$	$	$	$	$	$
Totals											
$	$	$	$	$	$	$	$	$	$	$	$
				Total Income	$					**Total Income**	$
-Monthly Expenses											**-Monthly Expenses**
$										$	
Monthly Budget										**Monthly Budget**	
$										$	
+Margin (left over)										**+Margin (left over)**	
$										$	

	Month				Year					
Expenses	**Day**	**Day**	**Day**	**Day**	**Day**	**Day**	**Day**	**Day**	**Day**	**Day**
Mortgage/ Rent	$	$	$	$	$	$	$	$	$	$
Electricity/ Gas	$	$	$	$	$	$	$	$	$	$
Water/trash	$	$	$	$	$	$	$	$	$	$
Internet/subscriptions	$	$	$	$	$	$	$	$	$	$
Auto insurance	$	$	$	$	$	$	$	$	$	$
Life insurance	$	$	$	$	$	$	$	$	$	$
Loans	$	$	$	$	$	$	$	$	$	$
Savings/ investment	$	$	$	$	$	$	$	$	$	$
Cell phone	$	$	$	$	$	$	$	$	$	$
Credit card	$	$	$	$	$	$	$	$	$	$
Transportation	$	$	$	$	$	$	$	$	$	$
Childcare	$	$	$	$	$	$	$	$	$	$
Groceries	$	$	$	$	$	$	$	$	$	$
Dining out	$	$	$	$	$	$	$	$	$	$
Clothing	$	$	$	$	$	$	$	$	$	$
Laundry/cleaning	$	$	$	$	$	$	$	$	$	$
Medical/prescriptions	$	$	$	$	$	$	$	$	$	$
Donations	$	$	$	$	$	$	$	$	$	$
Entertainment	$	$	$	$	$	$	$	$	$	$
Miscellaneous	$	$	$	$	$	$	$	$	$	$

Income 1		**Income 2**		**Additional Income**		**First Week**		**Second Week**		**Third Week**	
$	$	$	$	$	$	$	$	$	$	$	$
$	$	$	$	$	$	$	$	$	$	$	$
$	$	$	$	$	$	$	$	$	$	$	$
$	$	$	$	$	$	$	$	$	$	$	$
Totals											
$	$	$	$	$	$	$	$	$	$	$	$
				Total Income	$					**Total Income**	$
-Monthly Expenses											**-Monthly Expenses**
$										$	
Monthly Budget											**Monthly Budget**
$										$	
+Margin (left over)											**+Margin (left over)**
$										$	

	Month				Year					
Expenses	**Day**	**Day**	**Day**	**Day**	**Day**	**Day**	**Day**	**Day**	**Day**	**Day**
Mortgage/ Rent	$	$	$	$	$	$	$	$	$	$
Electricity/ Gas	$	$	$	$	$	$	$	$	$	$
Water/trash	$	$	$	$	$	$	$	$	$	$
Internet/subscriptions	$	$	$	$	$	$	$	$	$	$
Auto insurance	$	$	$	$	$	$	$	$	$	$
Life insurance	$	$	$	$	$	$	$	$	$	$
Loans	$	$	$	$	$	$	$	$	$	$
Savings/ investment	$	$	$	$	$	$	$	$	$	$
Cell phone	$	$	$	$	$	$	$	$	$	$
Credit card	$	$	$	$	$	$	$	$	$	$
Transportation	$	$	$	$	$	$	$	$	$	$
Childcare	$	$	$	$	$	$	$	$	$	$
Groceries	$	$	$	$	$	$	$	$	$	$
Dining out	$	$	$	$	$	$	$	$	$	$
Clothing	$	$	$	$	$	$	$	$	$	$
Laundry/cleaning	$	$	$	$	$	$	$	$	$	$
Medical/prescriptions	$	$	$	$	$	$	$	$	$	$
Donations	$	$	$	$	$	$	$	$	$	$
Entertainment	$	$	$	$	$	$	$	$	$	$
Miscellaneous	$	$	$	$	$	$	$	$	$	$

Income 1		**Income 2**		**Additional Income**		**First Week**		**Second Week**		**Third Week**	
$	$	$	$	$	$	$	$	$	$	$	$
$	$	$	$	$	$	$	$	$	$	$	$
$	$	$	$	$	$	$	$	$	$	$	$
$	$	$	$	$	$	$	$	$	$	$	$
					Totals						
$	$	$	$	$	$	$	$	$	$	$	$
				Total Income	$					**Total Income**	$
-Monthly Expenses										**-Monthly Expenses**	
$										$	
Monthly Budget										**Monthly Budget**	
$										$	
+Margin (left over)										**+Margin (left over)**	
$										$	

	Month				Year					
Expenses	**Day**	**Day**	**Day**	**Day**	**Day**	**Day**	**Day**	**Day**	**Day**	**Day**
Mortgage/ Rent	$	$	$	$	$	$	$	$	$	$
Electricity/ Gas	$	$	$	$	$	$	$	$	$	$
Water/trash	$	$	$	$	$	$	$	$	$	$
Internet/subscriptions	$	$	$	$	$	$	$	$	$	$
Auto insurance	$	$	$	$	$	$	$	$	$	$
Life insurance	$	$	$	$	$	$	$	$	$	$
Loans	$	$	$	$	$	$	$	$	$	$
Savings/ investment	$	$	$	$	$	$	$	$	$	$
Cell phone	$	$	$	$	$	$	$	$	$	$
Credit card	$	$	$	$	$	$	$	$	$	$
Transportation	$	$	$	$	$	$	$	$	$	$
Childcare	$	$	$	$	$	$	$	$	$	$
Groceries	$	$	$	$	$	$	$	$	$	$
Dining out	$	$	$	$	$	$	$	$	$	$
Clothing	$	$	$	$	$	$	$	$	$	$
Laundry/cleaning	$	$	$	$	$	$	$	$	$	$
Medical/prescriptions	$	$	$	$	$	$	$	$	$	$
Donations	$	$	$	$	$	$	$	$	$	$
Entertainment	$	$	$	$	$	$	$	$	$	$
Miscellaneous	$	$	$	$	$	$	$	$	$	$

Income 1		**Income 2**		**Additional Income**		**First Week**		**Second Week**		**Third Week**	
$	$	$	$	$	$	$	$	$	$	$	$
$	$	$	$	$	$	$	$	$	$	$	$
$	$	$	$	$	$	$	$	$	$	$	$
$	$	$	$	$	$	$	$	$	$	$	$
					Totals						
$	$	$	$	$	$	$	$	$	$	$	$
				Total Income	$					**Total Income**	$
-Monthly Expenses											**-Monthly Expenses**
$										$	
Monthly Budget											**Monthly Budget**
$										$	
+Margin (left over)											**+Margin (left over)**
$										$	

	Month				Year					
Expenses	**Day**	**Day**	**Day**	**Day**	**Day**	**Day**	**Day**	**Day**	**Day**	**Day**
Mortgage/ Rent	$	$	$	$	$	$	$	$	$	$
Electricity/ Gas	$	$	$	$	$	$	$	$	$	$
Water/trash	$	$	$	$	$	$	$	$	$	$
Internet/subscriptions	$	$	$	$	$	$	$	$	$	$
Auto insurance	$	$	$	$	$	$	$	$	$	$
Life insurance	$	$	$	$	$	$	$	$	$	$
Loans	$	$	$	$	$	$	$	$	$	$
Savings/ investment	$	$	$	$	$	$	$	$	$	$
Cell phone	$	$	$	$	$	$	$	$	$	$
Credit card	$	$	$	$	$	$	$	$	$	$
Transportation	$	$	$	$	$	$	$	$	$	$
Childcare	$	$	$	$	$	$	$	$	$	$
Groceries	$	$	$	$	$	$	$	$	$	$
Dining out	$	$	$	$	$	$	$	$	$	$
Clothing	$	$	$	$	$	$	$	$	$	$
Laundry/cleaning	$	$	$	$	$	$	$	$	$	$
Medical/prescriptions	$	$	$	$	$	$	$	$	$	$
Donations	$	$	$	$	$	$	$	$	$	$
Entertainment	$	$	$	$	$	$	$	$	$	$
Miscellaneous	$	$	$	$	$	$	$	$	$	$

Income 1		**Income 2**		**Additional Income**		**First Week**		**Second Week**		**Third Week**	
$	$	$	$	$	$	$	$	$	$	$	$
$	$	$	$	$	$	$	$	$	$	$	$
$	$	$	$	$	$	$	$	$	$	$	$
$	$	$	$	$	$	$	$	$	$	$	$
Totals											
$	$	$	$	$	$	$	$	$	$	$	$
				Total Income	$				**Total Income**		$
-Monthly Expenses										**-Monthly Expenses**	
$										$	
Monthly Budget										**Monthly Budget**	
$										$	
+Margin (left over)										**+Margin (left over)**	
$										$	

	Month				Year					
Expenses	**Day**	**Day**	**Day**	**Day**	**Day**	**Day**	**Day**	**Day**	**Day**	**Day**
Mortgage/ Rent	$	$	$	$	$	$	$	$	$	$
Electricity/ Gas	$	$	$	$	$	$	$	$	$	$
Water/trash	$	$	$	$	$	$	$	$	$	$
Internet/subscriptions	$	$	$	$	$	$	$	$	$	$
Auto insurance	$	$	$	$	$	$	$	$	$	$
Life insurance	$	$	$	$	$	$	$	$	$	$
Loans	$	$	$	$	$	$	$	$	$	$
Savings/ investment	$	$	$	$	$	$	$	$	$	$
Cell phone	$	$	$	$	$	$	$	$	$	$
Credit card	$	$	$	$	$	$	$	$	$	$
Transportation	$	$	$	$	$	$	$	$	$	$
Childcare	$	$	$	$	$	$	$	$	$	$
Groceries	$	$	$	$	$	$	$	$	$	$
Dining out	$	$	$	$	$	$	$	$	$	$
Clothing	$	$	$	$	$	$	$	$	$	$
Laundry/cleaning	$	$	$	$	$	$	$	$	$	$
Medical/prescriptions	$	$	$	$	$	$	$	$	$	$
Donations	$	$	$	$	$	$	$	$	$	$
Entertainment	$	$	$	$	$	$	$	$	$	$
Miscellaneous	$	$	$	$	$	$	$	$	$	$

Income 1		**Income 2**		**Additional Income**		**First Week**		**Second Week**		**Third Week**	
$	$	$	$	$	$	$	$	$	$	$	$
$	$	$	$	$	$	$	$	$	$	$	$
$	$	$	$	$	$	$	$	$	$	$	$
$	$	$	$	$	$	$	$	$	$	$	$
Totals											
$	$	$	$	$	$	$	$	$	$	$	$
Total Income					$					**Total Income**	$
-Monthly Expenses						**-Monthly Expenses**					
$										$	
Monthly Budget										**Monthly Budget**	
$										$	
+Margin (left over)										**+Margin (left over)**	
$										$	

	Month				Year					
Expenses	**Day**	**Day**	**Day**	**Day**	**Day**	**Day**	**Day**	**Day**	**Day**	**Day**
Mortgage/ Rent	$	$	$	$	$	$	$	$	$	$
Electricity/ Gas	$	$	$	$	$	$	$	$	$	$
Water/trash	$	$	$	$	$	$	$	$	$	$
Internet/subscriptions	$	$	$	$	$	$	$	$	$	$
Auto insurance	$	$	$	$	$	$	$	$	$	$
Life insurance	$	$	$	$	$	$	$	$	$	$
Loans	$	$	$	$	$	$	$	$	$	$
Savings/ investment	$	$	$	$	$	$	$	$	$	$
Cell phone	$	$	$	$	$	$	$	$	$	$
Credit card	$	$	$	$	$	$	$	$	$	$
Transportation	$	$	$	$	$	$	$	$	$	$
Childcare	$	$	$	$	$	$	$	$	$	$
Groceries	$	$	$	$	$	$	$	$	$	$
Dining out	$	$	$	$	$	$	$	$	$	$
Clothing	$	$	$	$	$	$	$	$	$	$
Laundry/cleaning	$	$	$	$	$	$	$	$	$	$
Medical/prescriptions	$	$	$	$	$	$	$	$	$	$
Donations	$	$	$	$	$	$	$	$	$	$
Entertainment	$	$	$	$	$	$	$	$	$	$
Miscellaneous	$	$	$	$	$	$	$	$	$	$

Income 1		**Income 2**		**Additional Income**		**First Week**		**Second Week**		**Third Week**	
$	$	$	$	$	$	$	$	$	$	$	$
$	$	$	$	$	$	$	$	$	$	$	$
$	$	$	$	$	$	$	$	$	$	$	$
$	$	$	$	$	$	$	$	$	$	$	$
Totals											
$	$	$	$	$	$	$	$	$	$	$	$
				Total Income	$				**Total Income**		$
-Monthly Expenses										**-Monthly Expenses**	
$										$	
Monthly Budget										**Monthly Budget**	
$										$	
+Margin (left over)										**+Margin (left over)**	
$										$	

	Month				Year					
Expenses	**Day**	**Day**	**Day**	**Day**	**Day**	**Day**	**Day**	**Day**	**Day**	**Day**
Mortgage/ Rent	$	$	$	$	$	$	$	$	$	$
Electricity/ Gas	$	$	$	$	$	$	$	$	$	$
Water/trash	$	$	$	$	$	$	$	$	$	$
Internet/subscriptions	$	$	$	$	$	$	$	$	$	$
Auto insurance	$	$	$	$	$	$	$	$	$	$
Life insurance	$	$	$	$	$	$	$	$	$	$
Loans	$	$	$	$	$	$	$	$	$	$
Savings/ investment	$	$	$	$	$	$	$	$	$	$
Cell phone	$	$	$	$	$	$	$	$	$	$
Credit card	$	$	$	$	$	$	$	$	$	$
Transportation	$	$	$	$	$	$	$	$	$	$
Childcare	$	$	$	$	$	$	$	$	$	$
Groceries	$	$	$	$	$	$	$	$	$	$
Dining out	$	$	$	$	$	$	$	$	$	$
Clothing	$	$	$	$	$	$	$	$	$	$
Laundry/cleaning	$	$	$	$	$	$	$	$	$	$
Medical/prescriptions	$	$	$	$	$	$	$	$	$	$
Donations	$	$	$	$	$	$	$	$	$	$
Entertainment	$	$	$	$	$	$	$	$	$	$
Miscellaneous	$	$	$	$	$	$	$	$	$	$

Income 1		**Income 2**		**Additional Income**		**First Week**		**Second Week**		**Third Week**	
$	$	$	$	$	$	$	$	$	$	$	$
$	$	$	$	$	$	$	$	$	$	$	$
$	$	$	$	$	$	$	$	$	$	$	$
$	$	$	$	$	$	$	$	$	$	$	$
Totals											
$	$	$	$	$	$	$	$	$	$	$	$
Total Income					$	**Total Income**					$
-Monthly Expenses						**-Monthly Expenses**					
$										$	
Monthly Budget										**Monthly Budget**	
$										$	
+Margin (left over)										**+Margin (left over)**	
$										$	

1 Year Plan Outline

Creating a one-year plan outline can help you focus on achieving personal, professional, or academic goals. Here's a simple structure that you can adapt based on your needs.

1. Vision and Purpose

Define your long-term vision.

Clarify why these goals are important to you.

What will achieving these goals contribute to your life or career?

2. Goal Setting

Identify key areas of your life (e.g., personal development, career, health, relationships).

Set 3-5 major goals for each area.

Example:

Career: Get promoted, develop new skills.

Health: Lose 10 lbs, run a half marathon.

Personal Development: Read 12 books, learn a new language.

3. Quarterly Breakdown (90-Day Milestones)

Divide your goals into quarterly segments to make progress more manageable.

Each quarter should have specific, measurable milestones that move you toward your goals.

Example:

Q1 (Jan - Mar): Complete a professional certification, establish a workout routine.

Q2 (Apr - Jun): Attend industry networking events, maintain exercise consistency.

Q3 (Jul - Sep): Take on leadership roles at work, reach a new fitness goal.

Q4 (Oct - Dec): Apply for a promotion, run a 10K race.

4. Monthly Objectives

Break down each quarterly milestone into monthly tasks.

Focus on specific, smaller achievements to stay on track.

Example:

January: Research and enroll in a certification course, create a 3-day workout plan.

February: Study and complete one module of the certification, increase workout intensity.

March: Take the certification exam, evaluate fitness progress.

5. Weekly Tasks

Outline weekly actions to ensure steady progress.

Keep a to-do list or habit tracker for daily accountability.

Example:

Week 1: Dedicate 5 hours to studying, exercise 3 times.

Week 2: Reach out to a mentor, review exam material.

6. Review and Adjust

Schedule regular reviews (monthly and quarterly) to track progress and make adjustments.

Reflect on what worked and what didn't.

Example:

End of Q1 Review: Assess certification progress, adjust workout routine.

End of Year: Reflect on goal achievement and personal growth.

7. Rewards and Motivation

Define how you'll celebrate when you hit key milestones.

Example:

Milestone 1: Celebrate by taking a weekend trip after completing a certification.

Milestone 2: Buy a new book after running the first 5K.

1 Year Plan Template

On a separate sheet of paper or on a word document, place your answers to the questions below.

1. Vision and Purpose

Vision: [What do you want to achieve over the next year?]

Purpose: [Why are these goals important to you? How will they impact your life/career?]

2. Goal Setting

Key Areas of Focus: [Choose 3-5 key areas like career, health, relationships, etc.]

Career: [e.g., Get promoted, learn a new skill]

Health: [e.g., Improve fitness, adopt a healthy diet]

Personal Development: [e.g., Learn a new language, read 12 books]

[Other Area]: [e.g., Improve relationships, save money]

3. Quarterly Breakdown (90-Day Milestones)

Q1 (Jan - Mar): [What will you achieve in the first 3 months?]

[Example: Complete a certification, start a new workout routine]

Q2 (Apr - Jun): [What will you achieve in the second quarter?]

[Example: Attend networking events, maintain fitness progress]

Q3 (Jul - Sep): [What will you achieve in the third quarter?]

[Example: Take on leadership roles, train for a 10K race]

Q4 (Oct - Dec): [What will you achieve in the last quarter?]

[Example: Apply for a promotion, achieve a fitness milestone]

4. Monthly Objectives

January: [List specific tasks for January]

February: [List specific tasks for February]

March: [List specific tasks for March]

April: [List specific tasks for April]

May: [List specific tasks for May]

June: [List specific tasks for June]

July: [List specific tasks for July]

August: [List specific tasks for August]

September: [List specific tasks for September]

October: [List specific tasks for October]

November: [List specific tasks for November]

December: [List specific tasks for December]

5. Weekly Tasks

Week 1: [What actions will you take this week?]

Week 2: [What actions will you take next week?]

Week 3: [What actions will you take the third week?]

Week 4: [What actions will you take the fourth week?]

6. Review and Adjust

Monthly Review:

January Review: [Reflect on January's progress]

February Review: [Reflect on February's progress]

[Repeat for all months]

Quarterly Review:

Q1 Review: [Assess progress made in Q1]

Q2 Review: [Assess progress made in Q2]

Q3 Review: [Assess progress made in Q3]

End-of-Year Review: [Reflect on what you accomplished this year, what you learned, and any changes you want to make moving forward]

7. Rewards and Motivation

Milestone 1 Reward: [Reward for hitting your first major milestone]

Milestone 2 Reward: [Reward for hitting your second major milestone]

Final Goal Celebration: [How will you celebrate your overall success after the year is complete?]

5-Year Plan Outline

1. Vision and Long-Term Purpose

Vision: [What do you want to achieve in 5 years?]

Purpose: [Why are these long-term goals important to you? What impact will they have on your future life, career, or personal development?]

2. Key Life Areas and Major Goals

Identify key areas of your life where you want to make progress. Set 1-2 major goals for each area to be achieved over 5 years.

Career/Professional: [e.g., Get a promotion, start a business, advance in your field]

Health & Wellness: [e.g., Reach a fitness level, build healthy habits, maintain a balanced lifestyle]

Personal Development: [e.g., Learn a new language, gain certifications, expand knowledge base]

Financial: [e.g., Save $X amount, invest in property, eliminate debt]

Relationships: [e.g., Build strong personal connections, grow a family, improve relationships]

3. 5-Year Goal Breakdown

Break your 5-year goals into annual milestones to make them manageable and measurable.

Year 1 (Short-term Focus)

Goal 1: [e.g., Start a side business, enroll in a certification course]

Goal 2: [e.g., Lose 10 lbs, start saving $X per month]

Year 2

Goal 1: [e.g., Achieve promotion or role change]

Goal 2: [e.g., Expand fitness routine, save enough for a down payment]

Year 3

Goal 1: [e.g., Launch business or take on major responsibilities]

Goal 2: [e.g., Reach a new financial milestone, further professional development]

Year 4

Goal 1: [e.g., Grow business or reach leadership role]

Goal 2: [e.g., Achieve major personal milestone (e.g., complete a degree)]

Year 5 (Long-term Results)

Goal 1: [e.g., Achieve financial freedom, grow career to target level]

Goal 2: [e.g., Build long-term healthy habits or finalize big projects]

4. Annual Goal Breakdown

Each year should be broken down into smaller goals to help track progress more closely.

Year 1

Quarter 1: [Set foundation for major goals, complete specific initial steps]

Quarter 2: [Continue progress with measurable outcomes, address any setbacks]

Quarter 3: [Ensure steady progress or reassess if adjustments are needed]

Quarter 4: [Reflect on the year and finalize any remaining goals for the year]

Repeat for Years 2-5.

5. Monthly & Weekly Breakdown

Monthly Objectives: Define specific objectives each month that contribute to your quarterly and yearly goals. These should be focused, measurable tasks.

Month 1: [Specific action steps]

Month 2: [Specific action steps]

Month 3: [Specific action steps]

Weekly Tasks: Break down the monthly objectives into weekly tasks to stay on track.

Week 1: [Action items]

Week 2: [Action items]

6. Mid-Year and Annual Reviews

Mid-Year Review (June/July of each year): Assess progress at the halfway point.

Questions to ask: What's working? What needs adjustment? Am I on track to reach my goals?

Annual Review (December): Reflect on the year's accomplishments, set goals for the next year, and make adjustments to the 5-year plan if necessary.

Questions to ask: What have I achieved? What obstacles did I face? What adjustments can I make?

7. Adjustments and Flexibility

Be open to adjusting your goals based on new opportunities, life changes, or unexpected obstacles. Flexibility is key to long-term planning.

8. Motivational Strategies and Rewards

Milestone 1 Reward: [Reward for achieving the first significant milestone (e.g., Year 1 goals)]

Milestone 2 Reward: [Reward for achieving a key Year 3 goal]

Final Celebration: [How will you celebrate the completion of your 5-year goals?]

5-Year Plan Template

On a separate sheet of paper or on a word document, place your answers to the questions below.

1. Vision and Long-Term Purpose

Vision: [What do you want to achieve in 5 years?]

Purpose: [Why are these long-term goals important to you? How will they impact your life/career/personal development?]

2. Key Life Areas and Major Goals

Set 1-2 major goals in each key area of your life to be achieved over the next 5 years.

Career/Professional: [e.g., Get a promotion, start a business, advance in your field]

Goal 1: [e.g., Start a business]

Goal 2: [e.g., Earn a promotion]

Health & Wellness: [e.g., Reach a fitness level, build healthy habits]

Goal 1: [e.g., Lose 20 pounds]

Goal 2: [e.g., Run a marathon]

Personal Development: [e.g., Learn a new skill, gain certifications]

Goal 1: [e.g., Become fluent in a new language]

Goal 2: [e.g., Read 30 books over 5 years]

Financial: [e.g., Save $X, eliminate debt]

Goal 1: [e.g., Save $50,000]

Goal 2: [e.g., Pay off student loans]

Relationships: [e.g., Improve personal connections, grow a family]

Goal 1: [e.g., Build stronger relationships with family]

Goal 2: [e.g., Cultivate a supportive social network]

3. 5-Year Goal Breakdown

Year 1 (Short-term Focus)

Goal 1: [e.g., Start a side business]

Goal 2: [e.g., Enroll in a certification course]

Year 2

Goal 1: [e.g., Earn a promotion]

Goal 2: [e.g., Reach 50% of my financial savings goal]

Year 3

Goal 1: [e.g., Launch a successful business]

Goal 2: [e.g., Achieve a fitness milestone (e.g., run a half marathon)]

Year 4

Goal 1: [e.g., Take on a leadership role at work]

Goal 2: [e.g., Reach full financial savings goal]

Year 5 (Long-term Results)

Goal 1: [e.g., Reach final career goal (e.g., top position or business expansion)]

Goal 2: [e.g., Achieve major personal milestone (e.g., complete marathon)]

4. Annual Goal Breakdown

For each year, break your goals into smaller tasks to be achieved each quarter.

Year 1

Quarter 1 (Jan-Mar): [e.g., Research business ideas, start fitness routine]

Quarter 2 (Apr-Jun): [e.g., Enroll in courses, save first $5,000]

Quarter 3 (Jul-Sep): [e.g., Launch website, maintain fitness consistency]

Quarter 4 (Oct-Dec): [e.g., Evaluate business progress, hit weight loss milestone]

Repeat for Years 2-5.

5. Monthly & Weekly Breakdown

Break down your quarterly goals into more specific monthly and weekly tasks for better tracking.

Monthly Objectives:

January: [e.g., Write business plan, run 5K]

February: [e.g., Apply for certification, increase savings contributions]

March: [e.g., Finalize business logistics, adjust workout routine]

Weekly Tasks:

Week 1: [Action steps like "Research business tools," "Exercise 3x per week"]

Week 2: [Continue with action items like "Create website," "Focus on healthy meals"]

6. Mid-Year and Annual Reviews

Mid-Year Review (June/July of each year): Assess progress at the halfway point.

Questions to ask: What's working? What needs adjustment? Am I on track to reach my goals?

Annual Review (December): Reflect on the year's accomplishments, set goals for the next year, and make adjustments as needed.

Questions to ask: What have I achieved this year? What obstacles did I face? What changes can I make to stay on track?

7. Adjustments and Flexibility

What new opportunities or challenges might impact your 5-year goals? How will you adapt?

8. Motivational Strategies and Rewards

Milestone 1 Reward (e.g., end of Year 1): [e.g., Treat yourself to a weekend getaway after launching your business]

Milestone 2 Reward (e.g., end of Year 3): [e.g., Buy something special after hitting a major fitness goal]

Final Celebration: [How will you celebrate after completing your 5-year plan?]

Financial Dictionary

1) **Accrual Accounting**: An accounting method that recognizes revenues and expenses when they are incurred or earned, regardless of when cash is exchanged. This method provides a more accurate representation of a company's financial performance over time.
2) **Accrued Interest**: The portion of interest income that has been earned but not yet received or paid to the investor. Accrued interest accumulates between coupon payment dates for fixed-income securities and is typically settled upon the next interest payment date or at the time of sale.
3) **Acquisition**: The process of one company purchasing or acquiring another company's assets, business operations, or controlling interest through a merger, stock purchase, or asset acquisition. Acquisitions are strategic transactions aimed at expanding market share, diversifying product offerings, or gaining synergies and efficiencies.
4) **Alpha**: A measure of an investment's performance relative to its benchmark index, adjusted for risk. Positive alpha indicates outperformance, while negative alpha suggests underperformance. Alpha is often used to assess the skill or value added by investment managers.
5) **Arbitrage**: The practice of simultaneously buying and selling assets or securities in different markets to take advantage of price discrepancies and earn risk-free profits. Arbitrageurs exploit inefficiencies in markets to bring prices back into equilibrium.
6) **Asset:** An asset is anything of value or a resource owned by an individual, corporation, or entity that can be converted into cash. Assets are the foundation of a company's or individual's balance sheet and contribute to their wealth. They can be tangible or intangible and are used to generate future economic benefits.
7) **Current Assets**: Assets that are expected to be converted to cash or used up within one year, such as cash, accounts receivable, and inventory.
8) **Fixed Assets (Tangible Assets):** Long-term assets used in the operation of a business, such as property, plant, and equipment (PP&E).
9) **Intangible Assets:** Non-physical assets, including patents, trademarks, copyrights, goodwill, and intellectual property.
10) **Financial Assets:** Investments like stocks, bonds, and cash equivalents that have a monetary value.
11) **Operating Assets**: Assets used in the day-to-day operations of a business, such as machinery and office supplies.
12) **Asset Allocation**: The process of distributing an investment portfolio among different asset classes, such as stocks, bonds, cash, and alternative investments, to achieve a desired risk-return profile. Asset allocation aims to optimize portfolio diversification and balance risk exposure.
13) **Asset Turnover Ratio**: A financial ratio that measures a company's efficiency in generating revenue from its assets by dividing its net sales or revenue by its average total assets. Asset turnover ratio indicates how effectively a company utilizes its assets to generate sales and is used to assess operational efficiency.
14) **Asset-Backed Security (ABS)**: A type of security that is collateralized by a pool of underlying assets, such as mortgages, auto loans, or credit card receivables. ABS issuers package these assets into securities and sell them to investors, with cash flows from the underlying assets used to pay interest and principal to investors.
15) **Backwardation**: A market condition in which the price of a futures contract is lower than the spot price of the underlying asset. Backwardation often occurs when there is an immediate shortage of the underlying asset or when the cost of carrying the asset is higher than the futures price.

16) **Bear Market Rally**: A temporary upward movement in stock prices or market indices within a longer-term bear market trend, characterized by pessimism, declining investor confidence, and overall market weakness. Bear market rallies may result from short-covering, technical factors, or speculative buying but often precede further declines.
17) **Bear Market**: A market condition characterized by declining stock prices, pessimism among investors, and a general expectation of further losses. Bear markets typically coincide with economic downturns and negative sentiment, lasting for an extended period.
18) **Benchmark Index**: A standard or reference index used to measure the performance of a specific market, asset class, sector, or investment strategy. Benchmark indices serve as benchmarks for evaluating the relative performance of investment portfolios and investment managers.
19) **Beta**: A measure of a stock's or portfolio's sensitivity to changes in the overall market or benchmark index, representing the systematic risk or volatility of the investment relative to the market. Beta values greater than 1 indicate higher volatility, while values less than 1 indicate lower volatility compared to the market.
20) **Black-Scholes Model**: A mathematical model used to calculate the theoretical price of European-style options, taking into account factors such as the price of the underlying asset, the option's strike price, time until expiration, volatility, and risk-free interest rate.
21) **Blue Chip Stocks**: Stocks of large, well-established companies with a history of stable earnings, strong financials, and a reputable brand presence. Blue chip stocks are considered relatively safe investments and are often included in diversified portfolios for long-term growth and income.
22) **Bond Duration**: A measure of the sensitivity of a bond's price to changes in interest rates, representing the weighted average time it takes for the bond's cash flows to be received. Duration helps investors assess the interest rate risk associated with bond investments.
23) **Call Option**: A financial contract that gives the holder the right, but not the obligation, to buy a specified amount of an underlying asset at a predetermined price within a specified time frame.
24) **Callable Bond**: A type of bond that allows the issuer to redeem or "call" the bond before its maturity date, typically at a predetermined price known as the call price. Callable bonds give the issuer flexibility to refinance debt at lower interest rates or to adjust the capital structure as needed.
25) **Callable Preferred Stock**: A type of preferred stock that gives the issuing company the right to redeem or "call" the shares at a predetermined price after a specified call date. Callable preferred stock provides flexibility to the issuer but may result in early redemption for investors if interest rates decline.
26) **Candlestick Chart**: A type of financial chart used to visualize price movements in a security or financial instrument over a specified period. Candlestick charts display open, high, low, and closing prices for each time interval, with candlestick patterns used to analyze market sentiment and trends.
27) **Capital Adequacy Ratio (CAR)**: A measure of a bank's capital relative to its risk-weighted assets, used to assess its financial stability and ability to absorb losses.
28) **Capital Adequacy**: The measure of a bank's financial strength and ability to withstand adverse events or losses while maintaining operations and meeting regulatory requirements. Capital adequacy is assessed based on the bank's capital levels, risk-weighted assets, and regulatory capital ratios.
29) **Capital Asset Pricing Model (CAPM)**: A financial model that describes the relationship between risk and expected return, used to estimate the expected return on an investment based on its risk profile and the risk-free rate of return.
30) **Capital Flight**: The rapid outflow of capital from a country due to concerns about economic or political stability, often resulting in currency depreciation and financial instability.

31) **Capital Gains Tax**: A tax imposed on the profit realized from the sale or disposition of capital assets, such as stocks, bonds, real estate, or collectibles. Capital gains tax rates vary based on the holding period of the asset and the taxpayer's income tax bracket, with long-term capital gains taxed at lower rates than short-term gains.
32) **Capital Gains**: Profits from the sale of assets or investments, such as stocks or real estate.
33) **Capital Market**: The market for buying and selling long-term debt and equity instruments, such as stocks and bonds.
34) **Capital Structure**: The mix of debt and equity financing used by a company to fund its operations and investments. Capital structure decisions involve determining the optimal balance between debt and equity to minimize the cost of capital and maximize shareholder value.
35) **Cash Flow Statement**: A financial statement that reports the cash inflows and outflows from a company's operating, investing, and financing activities over a specific period. The cash flow statement provides insights into a company's liquidity, solvency, and ability to generate cash to meet its obligations and fund growth.
36) **Collateralized Debt Obligation (CDO)**: A complex financial product backed by a pool of debt securities, such as mortgages or corporate bonds, divided into tranches with varying levels of risk and return.
37) **Collateralized Loan Obligation (CLO)**: A type of asset-backed security that pools together a portfolio of leveraged loans, typically made to corporate borrowers with below-investment-grade credit ratings. CLOs divide the cash flows from the underlying loans into tranches with varying levels of risk and return.
38) **Contingent Convertible (CoCo) Bond**: A type of hybrid security that combines features of both debt and equity instruments, with the potential to convert into common equity or be written down in the event of predefined triggers, such as the issuer's financial distress or regulatory capital breaches.
39) **Convertible Bond Arbitrage**: A trading strategy that seeks to profit from pricing discrepancies between a convertible bond and its underlying stock. Convertible bond arbitrageurs buy the convertible bond while simultaneously short-selling the underlying stock to hedge against price movements and capture the convertible bond's embedded option value.
40) **Convertible Bond**: A type of corporate bond that can be converted into a predetermined number of shares of the issuer's common stock at the bondholder's discretion.
41) **Convertible Preferred Stock**: A type of preferred stock that can be converted into a predetermined number of common shares of the issuing company at the discretion of the shareholder, typically at a specified conversion ratio.
42) **Convertible Securities**: Financial instruments, such as convertible bonds or convertible preferred stock, that can be exchanged for a predetermined number of common shares of the issuing company at the holder's discretion.
43) **Corporate Governance**: The system of rules, practices, and processes by which a company is directed and controlled, encompassing the relationships between management, shareholders, the board of directors, and other stakeholders. Effective corporate governance aims to promote transparency, accountability, and integrity in corporate decision-making.
44) **Cost of Capital**: The required rate of return that a company must achieve to justify the cost of raising funds through equity, debt, or other sources. It represents the opportunity cost of using capital for a particular investment.
45) **Counterparty Risk**: The risk that a party to a financial transaction will default on its obligations, leaving the other party exposed to financial losses. Counterparty risk is particularly relevant in over-the-counter (OTC) derivatives markets and in transactions with less creditworthy counterparties.

46) **Credit Default Swap (CDS)**: A financial derivative contract that provides protection against the default of a borrower or issuer of debt securities, with the buyer paying a premium to the seller in exchange for compensation in the event of default.
47) **Credit Rating**: An assessment of the creditworthiness of a borrower or issuer of debt securities, assigned by credit rating agencies based on factors such as financial strength, repayment history, and economic outlook.
48) **Dark Pool**: A private electronic trading venue or exchange where institutional investors can anonymously trade large blocks of securities away from public exchanges, reducing market impact and minimizing information leakage.
49) **Debenture**: A type of debt instrument issued by corporations or governments that is backed only by the issuer's general creditworthiness and reputation, rather than by specific collateral.
50) **Debt Service Coverage Ratio (DSCR)**: A financial ratio used to evaluate a company's ability to meet its debt obligations by comparing its operating income to its total debt service requirements, including interest and principal payments. DSCR measures the company's capacity to generate sufficient cash flow to cover its debt obligations.
51) **Debtor-in-Possession (DIP) Financing**: Financing provided to a company that has filed for bankruptcy protection under Chapter 11 of the U.S. Bankruptcy Code, allowing the company to continue operating while restructuring its debts. DIP financing is typically secured by the company's assets and has priority over existing debt obligations.
52) **Default Rate**: The percentage of loans or bonds in a portfolio that fail to meet their contractual payment obligations, typically expressed as an annualized rate. Default rates are used to assess credit risk and evaluate the performance of fixed-income investments.
53) **Default Risk**: The risk that a borrower will fail to meet its obligations, such as interest or principal payments, on a debt instrument. It is commonly associated with bonds or loans issued by companies or governments.
54) **Deflation**: A sustained decrease in the general price level of goods and services in an economy, often accompanied by reduced consumer spending, lower business investment, and increased unemployment.
55) **Derivative**: A financial contract whose value is derived from the performance of an underlying asset, index, or entity.
56) **Dilution**: The decrease in the ownership percentage of existing shareholders in a company due to the issuance of additional shares, typically through a secondary offering, convertible securities conversion, or stock-based compensation.
57) **Diversification**: Spreading investments across different assets or asset classes to reduce risk.
58) **Dividend Aristocrat**: A company that has consistently increased its dividend payments to shareholders for a specified number of consecutive years, typically 25 years or more. Dividend aristocrats are considered reliable income investments and often have strong track records of financial stability and growth.
59) **Dividend Discount Model (DDM)**: A method for valuing a company's stock by estimating the present value of its future dividend payments.
60) **Dividend Payout Ratio**: A financial ratio that measures the proportion of a company's earnings paid out to shareholders in the form of dividends. Dividend payout ratio is calculated by dividing total dividends by net income and is used to assess a company's dividend policy and sustainability.
61) **Dividend Reinvestment Plan (DRIP)**: A program offered by companies that allows shareholders to automatically reinvest dividends received from the company's stock into additional shares, often at a discount to the market price. DRIPs enable investors to compound their returns over time and accumulate more shares without paying brokerage fees.

62) **Dividend Yield**: A financial ratio that indicates the annual dividend income earned per share relative to the price per share of a stock. It is calculated by dividing the annual dividend per share by the current market price per share.
63) **Dividend**: A portion of a company's earnings distributed to shareholders, usually in cash or additional shares.
64) **Duration Matching**: An immunization strategy used by bond investors to match the duration of their bond portfolios with their investment time horizon or liability duration. Duration matching helps investors manage interest rate risk and stabilize the value of their portfolios.
65) **Earnings Per Share (EPS)**: A financial metric that represents the portion of a company's profit allocated to each outstanding share of common stock, calculated by dividing the company's net income by its total number of shares outstanding. EPS is used to assess a company's profitability and is a key factor in determining its stock valuation.
66) **Economic Indicator**: Data points used to gauge the health and direction of an economy, such as GDP growth, unemployment rate, consumer spending, and inflation.
67) **Economic Indicators**: Statistical data or metrics that provide insights into the overall health and performance of an economy, including measures of economic activity, employment, inflation, consumer spending, and business confidence. Economic indicators are used by policymakers, investors, and analysts to assess economic trends and make informed decisions.
68) **Economic Value Added (EVA)**: A financial performance metric that measures the difference between a company's net operating profit after taxes (NOPAT) and its cost of capital. EVA is used to assess a company's value creation relative to the capital invested and is considered a measure of shareholder wealth creation.
69) **Efficient Market Hypothesis (EMH)**: A theory that asserts that financial markets are efficient and that asset prices reflect all available information, making it impossible to consistently outperform the market.
70) **Emerging Market**: A term used to describe economies that are transitioning from developing to developed status and typically exhibit rapid economic growth, industrialization, and urbanization. Emerging markets often present investment opportunities but also carry higher levels of political, economic, and financial risk compared to developed markets.
71) **Equity Capital**: Funds raised by a company through the sale of shares of common or preferred stock to investors. It represents ownership in the company and is used to finance operations, investments, and growth initiatives.
72) **Equity Financing**: The process of raising capital by selling ownership stakes or equity shares in a company to investors, rather than borrowing funds through debt instruments. Equity financing allows companies to raise funds without incurring debt obligations but involves diluting ownership and sharing future profits with shareholders.
73) **Equity Risk Premium (ERP)**: The excess return that investors demand for investing in stocks over the risk-free rate of return, representing compensation for the higher risk associated with equity investments.
74) **Equity Risk Premium**: The excess return that investors expect to earn from investing in stocks or equity securities compared to risk-free assets, such as government bonds or Treasury bills. Equity risk premium reflects the compensation investors demand for bearing the higher risk and volatility associated with equities.
75) **Exchange-Traded Fund (ETF)**: A type of investment fund that tracks the performance of a specific index, sector, commodity, or asset class and trades on a stock exchange like an individual stock. ETFs offer diversification, liquidity, and transparency to investors at a low cost.
76) **Ex-Dividend Date**: The date on which a stock begins trading without the right to receive the next dividend payment. Investors who purchase shares on or after the ex-dividend date are not

entitled to receive the upcoming dividend, which is typically paid to shareholders of record as of the dividend record date.

77) **Fair Market Value (FMV)**: The price at which an asset would sell between a willing buyer and a willing seller in an open and unrestricted market, with both parties having reasonable knowledge of the relevant facts and neither being under compulsion to buy or sell.
78) **Fair Value Accounting**: An accounting method that measures the value of assets and liabilities based on their current market prices or estimated market values, rather than historical cost. It aims to provide a more accurate reflection of a company's financial position.
79) **Federal Open Market Committee (FOMC)**: The monetary policymaking body of the Federal Reserve System responsible for setting the target range for the federal funds rate and implementing monetary policy to achieve the Fed's dual mandate of price stability and maximum employment. The FOMC meets regularly to assess economic conditions and adjust monetary policy as needed.
80) **Financial Derivative**: A financial instrument whose value is derived from the value of an underlying asset, index, or reference rate.
81) **Financial Engineering**: The application of mathematical and quantitative techniques to design, create, and manage complex financial products, structures, or solutions. Financial engineers use tools from mathematics, statistics, and computer science to innovate and optimize financial processes and instruments.
82) **Financial Intermediary**: An institution or individual that acts as a middleman between savers and borrowers in the financial system, facilitating the flow of funds from surplus to deficit units through channels such as banks, insurance companies, and mutual funds.
83) **Financial Leverage**: The use of debt or borrowed funds to finance investments or operations, with the aim of magnifying returns to equity investors. Financial leverage amplifies both gains and losses and can increase the risk and volatility of investment portfolios.
84) **Financial Market Infrastructure (FMI)**: The infrastructure comprising systems, institutions, and arrangements that facilitate the clearing, settlement, and custody of financial transactions, including payment systems, central counterparties (CCPs), securities depositories, and central securities clearinghouses.
85) **Financial Ratios**: Quantitative metrics used to evaluate the financial performance, health, and efficiency of a company, calculated by comparing different financial variables or line items from the company's financial statements. Common financial ratios include profitability ratios, liquidity ratios, solvency ratios, and efficiency ratios.
86) **Financial Statement Analysis**: The process of analyzing and interpreting a company's financial statements to assess its financial performance, liquidity, solvency, and profitability.
87) **Fiscal Policy**: Government policy concerning taxation and spending, aimed at influencing the economy.
88) **Fixed-Income Securities**: Financial instruments that pay a fixed or predictable stream of income to investors, such as bonds, Treasury securities, and certificates of deposit (CDs). Fixed-income securities are typically less volatile than stocks and are often used to generate income and preserve capital.
89) **Foreign Exchange Market (Forex)**: The global marketplace where currencies are traded against each other, facilitating international trade and investment. It is the largest and most liquid financial market in the world.
90) **Futures Contract**: A standardized financial contract between two parties to buy or sell an asset (such as commodities, currencies, or financial instruments) at a future date and price agreed upon today.
91) **Gross Domestic Product (GDP)**: The total value of all goods and services produced within a country's borders over a specific period, typically measured on a quarterly or annual basis. GDP is a key indicator of a country's economic performance and growth trajectory.

92) **Gross Domestic Product (GDP)**: The total value of all goods and services produced within a country's borders over a specified period, typically measured on a quarterly or annual basis. GDP is a key indicator of a country's economic performance and growth trajectory.

93) **Growth Investing**: An investment strategy that focuses on selecting stocks or assets expected to grow at an above-average rate compared to the overall market or industry peers. Growth investors typically seek companies with strong earnings growth, innovative products or services, and expanding market opportunities.

94) **Growth Stock**: A stock of a company that is expected to grow at an above-average rate compared to its industry peers or the overall market, typically characterized by strong revenue growth, earnings potential, and market expansion opportunities. Growth stocks often trade at higher valuations and may pay lower dividends.

95) **Hedge Fund**: A pooled investment vehicle that employs various investment strategies, including long and short positions, leverage, derivatives, and alternative assets, to generate returns for sophisticated investors. Hedge funds typically target absolute returns and may use hedging techniques to manage risk.

96) **Hedge Ratio**: The ratio of the size of a hedging position to the size of the exposure being hedged, used to determine the appropriate amount of hedging needed to offset risk. Hedge ratios are calculated based on factors such as volatility, correlation, and market conditions.

97) **Hedge**: A strategy used to reduce or offset the risk of adverse price movements in an asset or portfolio.

98) **High-Frequency Trading (HFT)**: A form of algorithmic trading characterized by the use of sophisticated computer algorithms and high-speed data connections to execute large numbers of trades in milliseconds or microseconds. HFT strategies aim to exploit small price discrepancies and market inefficiencies for short-term profits.

99) **High-Yield Bond**: A bond issued by a company with below-investment-grade credit ratings, typically rated below BBB by credit rating agencies. High-yield bonds offer higher yields to compensate investors for the increased risk of default compared to investment-grade bonds.

100) **Hurdle Rate**: The minimum rate of return or threshold required by an investor or company to justify an investment decision, undertake a project, or accept a business opportunity. Hurdle rates are used to evaluate the feasibility and profitability of investments and ensure that they meet predefined investment criteria.

101) **Inflation Hedge**: An investment or asset class that tends to maintain or increase its value over time in periods of inflation, providing a hedge against the erosion of purchasing power. Inflation hedges include commodities, real estate, inflation-protected securities, and certain alternative investments.

102) **Inflation Rate**: The rate at which the general level of prices for goods and services is rising within an economy over a certain period of time, typically measured as an annual percentage increase.

103) **Inflation-Protected Securities (IPS)**: Fixed-income securities, such as Treasury Inflation-Protected Securities (TIPS), that offer protection against inflation by adjusting their principal value and interest payments based on changes in the Consumer Price Index (CPI) or other inflation measures. IPS provide investors with a hedge against purchasing power erosion caused by inflation.

104) **Inflation-Protected Securities (TIPS)**: Government bonds or securities that are indexed to inflation, providing investors with protection against purchasing power erosion due to inflation by adjusting the bond's principal value and interest payments based on changes in the Consumer Price Index (CPI).

105) **Initial Margin**: The amount of collateral required by a broker or clearinghouse from an investor to cover potential losses on a futures or options contract. Initial margin is calculated

based on the contract's current market value and represents a percentage of the total contract value.

106) **Initial Margin**: The amount of collateral required by a broker or clearinghouse from an investor to cover potential losses on a futures or options contract. Initial margin is calculated based on the contract's current market value and represents a percentage of the total contract value.

107) **Initial Public Offering (IPO)**: The process by which a private company offers shares of its stock to the public for the first time, allowing investors to purchase ownership stakes in the company. IPOs provide companies with access to capital markets and liquidity for existing shareholders.

108) **Insolvency**: A financial state in which an individual or entity is unable to meet its financial obligations and liabilities as they come due.

109) **Interest Rate Swaps**: A financial derivative contract between two parties to exchange fixed-rate and floating-rate interest payments over a specified period. Interest rate swaps are used by companies, financial institutions, and investors to manage interest rate risk and adjust their debt exposure.

110) **Intrinsic Value**: The calculated or estimated value of an asset based on its fundamental characteristics and cash flow potential. It is used in various valuation models to determine whether an asset is undervalued or overvalued.

111) **Joint and Several Liability**: A legal principle that holds multiple parties jointly and individually liable for the full amount of a debt, obligation, or damages, allowing the creditor or claimant to pursue any or all of the parties to recover the entire amount owed. Joint and several liability provides creditors with greater protection and recourse in case of default or non-payment.

112) **Joint Venture (JV)**: A business arrangement in which two or more parties collaborate to undertake a specific project, venture, or business activity, sharing risks, resources, and rewards. Joint ventures are often formed to pursue opportunities that require specialized expertise, capital, or access to markets.

113) **Junk Bond**: A high-yield or speculative bond issued by a company with below-investment-grade credit ratings, typically rated BB or lower by credit rating agencies. Junk bonds offer higher yields to compensate investors for the increased risk of default compared to investment-grade bonds.

114) **Key Performance Indicator (KPI)**: A quantifiable measure used to evaluate the performance or success of an organization, department, project, or individual against specific objectives or goals. KPIs are commonly used in business management to monitor progress, identify areas for improvement, and drive decision-making.

115) **Kurtosis**: A statistical measure that quantifies the degree of peakedness or flatness of the probability distribution of a random variable, relative to a normal distribution. Positive kurtosis indicates a sharper peak and heavier tails, while negative kurtosis indicates a flatter peak and lighter tails.

116) **Lender of Last Resort**: A central bank or other financial institution that provides emergency funding or liquidity support to financial institutions facing solvency or liquidity crises. Lenders of last resort aim to maintain financial stability and prevent systemic disruptions in the financial system.

117) **Leverage Ratio**: A financial ratio that measures the proportion of a company's debt to its equity capital, indicating the extent to which the company is financed by debt. Leverage ratios are used to assess a company's financial risk and solvency, with higher leverage ratios indicating higher financial leverage.

118) **Leverage**: The use of borrowed funds to increase the potential return of an investment.

119) **Leveraged Buyout (LBO)**: A corporate finance transaction in which a company is acquired using a significant amount of borrowed funds or leverage, with the target company's assets serving as collateral for the debt. LBOs are often undertaken by private equity firms to acquire, restructure, and eventually sell or take public target companies.

120) **Liquidity Preference Theory**: A theory that suggests investors prefer to hold assets in the most liquid form, such as cash or short-term securities, to meet their liquidity needs. According to this theory, investors demand higher returns for holding less liquid assets, leading to an upward-sloping yield curve.

121) **Liquidity Preference**: The tendency of investors to prefer holding liquid assets, such as cash, money market instruments, or highly liquid securities, over less liquid investments, due to uncertainty, risk aversion, or the need for short-term liquidity. Liquidity preference influences asset prices and market dynamics.

122) **Liquidity Risk**: The risk that an asset cannot be bought or sold quickly enough in the market without significantly affecting its price, potentially resulting in losses or reduced returns for investors.

123) **Liquidity Risk**: The risk that an investment or asset cannot be sold or converted into cash quickly and at a fair price, resulting in losses or financial difficulties for the investor. Liquidity risk arises from factors such as market illiquidity, trading restrictions, or sudden changes in investor sentiment.

124) **Liquidity Trap**: A situation in which interest rates are very low, and monetary policy measures such as central bank interventions fail to stimulate economic growth or inflation. Liquidity traps occur when consumers and businesses hoard cash rather than spend or invest, leading to stagnant economic activity.

125) **Liquidity**: The degree to which an asset or security can be quickly bought or sold in the market without affecting its price.

126) **Margin Call**: A demand from a broker or lender for additional funds or collateral to cover potential losses on an investment or trading position that has moved against the investor. Margin calls occur when the value of the collateral falls below a certain threshold, requiring the investor to deposit more funds or close out the position.

127) **Margin Trading**: A trading strategy that involves borrowing funds from a broker to purchase securities, using the securities as collateral. Margin trading allows investors to amplify their potential returns but also increases the risk of losses and margin calls if the market moves against them.

128) **Margin**: The amount of funds required to open and maintain a leveraged position in a financial market.

129) **Market Capitalization (Market Cap)**: The total value of a company's outstanding shares of common stock, calculated by multiplying the current market price per share by the total number of shares outstanding. Market capitalization is used to classify companies by size (e.g., large-cap, mid-cap, small-cap) and is a key determinant of stock indices and investment benchmarks.

130) **Market Capitalization Weighted Index**: A stock market index in which the constituent companies are weighted based on their market capitalization, with larger companies having a greater impact on the index's performance.

131) **Market Capitalization**: The total value of a company's outstanding shares of stock, calculated by multiplying the share price by the number of shares outstanding.

132) **Market Efficiency**: The degree to which prices of financial assets reflect all available information and are therefore accurately priced.

133) **Market Maker**: A financial institution or individual that stands ready to buy and sell securities in a particular market, providing liquidity and facilitating trading by maintaining bid and ask prices.

134) **Market Order**: An order to buy or sell a security at the current market price, executed immediately.

135) **Mark-to-Market**: The process of valuing assets or liabilities based on their current market prices, used to determine the fair value of financial instruments for accounting and reporting purposes.

136) **Maturity Date**: The date on which a debt security, such as a bond or certificate of deposit (CD), becomes due and payable, at which point the principal amount is repaid to the investor.

137) **Maturity Transformation**: A process by which financial intermediaries, such as banks or mutual funds, borrow funds on a short-term basis and lend them out on a long-term basis, earning a spread between the short-term borrowing rate and the long-term lending rate. Maturity transformation is a key function of banks and helps match the maturities of assets and liabilities.

138) **Maturity Transformation**: The process by which financial intermediaries, such as banks or mutual funds, borrow funds on a short-term basis and lend them out on a long-term basis, earning a spread between short-term borrowing rates and long-term lending rates. Maturity transformation is a key function of banks and helps match the maturities of assets and liabilities.

139) **Monetary Policy Transmission Mechanism**: The process through which changes in a central bank's monetary policy, such as interest rate adjustments or open market operations, influence economic variables such as inflation, output, and employment. The transmission mechanism typically operates through channels such as interest rates, exchange rates, credit availability, and asset prices.

140) **Monetary Policy**: The actions of a central bank, such as interest rate adjustments, aimed at controlling inflation and promoting economic growth.

141) **Moral Hazard**: The risk that individuals or institutions may take excessive risks or engage in irresponsible behavior when they are insulated from the consequences of their actions, often due to the presence of insurance, bailouts, or government guarantees. Moral hazard can lead to market distortions and systemic risks.

142) **Mortgage-backed Security (MBS)**: A type of asset-backed security that is secured by a bundle of mortgage loans.

143) **Mutual Fund**: An investment vehicle that pools money from multiple investors to invest in a diversified portfolio of stocks, bonds, or other securities, managed by professional fund managers.

144) **Naked Option**: An options trading strategy in which an investor sells options contracts without owning the underlying asset or holding a corresponding position to hedge the risk. Naked options expose the seller to unlimited potential losses and are considered speculative and high-risk.

145) **Net Asset Value (NAV)**: The per-share value of a mutual fund, ETF, or investment trust, calculated by dividing the total net assets of the fund by the number of shares outstanding. NAV represents the intrinsic value of the fund's underlying assets and is typically calculated at the end of each trading day.

146) **Net Present Value (NPV)**: A financial metric used to evaluate the profitability of an investment or project by calculating the present value of its expected future cash flows, discounted at an appropriate discount rate. NPV compares the value of cash inflows to the

initial investment and helps assess whether an investment generates positive or negative returns.

147) **Net Working Capital (NWC)**: The difference between a company's current assets and current liabilities, representing the amount of capital available to fund day-to-day operations and short-term liquidity needs. Net working capital is used to assess a company's short-term financial health and operating efficiency.

148) **Operating Lease**: A lease agreement in which the lessee (tenant) is granted the right to use an asset, such as equipment or real estate, for a specified period of time in exchange for periodic lease payments. Operating leases are typically shorter-term and do not transfer ownership of the asset to the lessee.

149) **Operating Margin**: A financial ratio that measures the profitability of a company's core business operations by dividing its operating income by its net sales or revenue. Operating margin reflects the efficiency of a company in generating profits from its primary business activities, excluding non-operating expenses and income.

150) **Operational Risk**: The risk of loss resulting from inadequate or failed internal processes, systems, or controls, human error, or external events, such as natural disasters or cyberattacks.

151) **Option Greeks**: A set of risk measures used to assess the sensitivity of options prices to changes in various factors, including underlying asset price, volatility, time to expiration, interest rates, and dividends. Option Greeks include delta, gamma, theta, vega, and rho, and help investors manage option positions and risks.

152) **Out-of-the-Money (OTM)**: A term used to describe an options contract that has no intrinsic value because the underlying asset's price is below the strike price for call options or above the strike price for put options. Out-of-the-money options are speculative and carry higher risk but may offer leverage and potential returns if the underlying asset's price moves favorably.

153) **Over the Counter (OTC) Market**: A decentralized financial market where securities are traded directly between buyers and sellers, outside of traditional stock exchanges. OTC markets include securities that are not listed on formal exchanges and may involve negotiated transactions or electronic trading platforms.

154) **Passive Investing**: An investment strategy that seeks to replicate the performance of a broad market index or benchmark, such as the S&P 500, by investing in a diversified portfolio of securities with low turnover and minimal management. Passive investors typically utilize index funds or exchange-traded funds (ETFs) to achieve market exposure.

155) **Penny Stock**: A low-priced stock typically traded over the counter (OTC) or on small-cap exchanges, often with limited liquidity and market capitalization. Penny stocks are characterized by their high volatility and speculative nature, and they may lack regulatory oversight compared to stocks listed on major exchanges.

156) **Ponzi Scheme**: A fraudulent investment scheme that pays returns to investors from their own money or from the money of new investors, rather than from profit earned by the individual or organization running the scheme.

157) **Portfolio Diversification**: A risk management strategy that involves spreading investments across multiple asset classes, sectors, industries, and geographic regions to reduce the impact of individual asset price movements on overall portfolio performance. Portfolio diversification aims to minimize risk while maximizing returns.

158) **Preferred Stock**: A class of ownership in a corporation that typically has priority over common stock in terms of dividends and liquidation preferences but may not carry voting rights. Preferred stock combines features of debt and equity securities and offers investors fixed dividends and potentially higher yields than common stock.

159) **Price Discovery**: The process by which market participants determine the fair market value of a security, commodity, or financial instrument based on supply and demand dynamics, trading activity, and information dissemination. Price discovery facilitates efficient markets and ensures that asset prices reflect all available information.

160) **Principal Component Analysis (PCA)**: A statistical technique used to reduce the dimensionality of data by identifying and extracting the most important patterns or components from a dataset. PCA is commonly used in finance for risk management, portfolio optimization, and factor analysis.

161) **Private Equity (PE)**: Equity capital invested in privately held companies or in public companies that are taken private through leveraged buyouts (LBOs). Private equity investors typically seek to acquire or invest in companies with growth potential and improve their performance over time before exiting through a sale or public offering.

162) **Private Placement**: The sale of securities to a select group of investors in a private offering, bypassing the public markets and regulatory requirements associated with public offerings. Private placements are typically used by companies to raise capital from institutional investors, accredited investors, or venture capital firms.

163) **Purchasing Power Parity (PPP)**: A theory that suggests exchange rates between currencies will adjust to ensure that identical goods cost the same in different countries when the prices are expressed in the same currency.

164) **Put Option**: A financial contract that gives the holder the right, but not the obligation, to sell a specified amount of an underlying asset at a predetermined price within a specified time frame.

165) **Qualified Dividend**: A dividend paid by a U.S. corporation or qualified foreign corporation that qualifies for favorable tax treatment under the Internal Revenue Code. Qualified dividends are taxed at capital gains rates rather than ordinary income tax rates for eligible investors.

166) **Quantitative Analysis**: The use of mathematical and statistical techniques to analyze financial data, model complex relationships, and make informed investment decisions. Quantitative analysts, or quants, develop mathematical models, algorithms, and trading strategies to exploit market inefficiencies and generate alpha.

167) **Quantitative Easing (QE)**: A monetary policy tool used by central banks to stimulate the economy by purchasing government securities or other assets from the market, increasing the money supply and lowering long-term interest rates. QE aims to boost lending, investment, and economic activity during periods of low inflation or recession.

168) **Quantitative Tightening (QT)**: The process of reducing the size of a central bank's balance sheet and withdrawing liquidity from the financial system by selling or allowing maturing securities to roll off without reinvestment. QT is used by central banks to normalize monetary policy and remove excess liquidity accumulated during quantitative easing (QE) programs.

169) **Real Estate Investment Trust (REIT)**: A company that owns, operates, or finances income-generating real estate assets, such as office buildings, shopping malls, or apartment complexes, and distributes the majority of its taxable income to shareholders in the form of dividends. REITs offer investors exposure to real estate with the liquidity of publicly traded stocks.

170) **Real Options**: A strategic investment approach that applies the principles of financial options theory to assess and evaluate the value of managerial flexibility and strategic decision-making opportunities in business projects or investments. Real options analysis helps managers quantify and manage uncertainty and risk in dynamic environments.

171) **Realized Gain/Loss**: The actual profit or loss realized by an investor from the sale or disposition of an investment, calculated as the difference between the selling price and the purchase price, adjusted for transaction costs, taxes, and other expenses. Realized gains/losses are reported on tax returns and financial statements.

172) **Rebalancing**: The process of adjusting the allocation of assets in an investment portfolio to bring it back to its target asset allocation, typically done periodically to maintain desired risk levels and investment objectives.

173) **Recession**: A significant decline in economic activity that lasts for an extended period, typically marked by a decrease in GDP, employment, and consumer spending.

174) **Regression Analysis**: A statistical technique used to examine the relationship between two or more variables, often employed in financial modeling and forecasting.

175) **Reinvestment Risk**: The risk that future cash flows from an investment will be reinvested at a lower rate of return, resulting in lower overall returns than expected.

176) **Repo Rate**: The rate at which the central bank lends money to commercial banks for the short term, using repurchase agreements (repos) as collateral.

177) **Return on Equity (ROE)**: A financial ratio that measures the profitability of a company's equity investment by dividing its net income by its shareholders' equity. ROE indicates the efficiency with which a company generates profits from shareholders' investments and is used to assess management's ability to deploy capital effectively.

178) **Return on Investment (ROI)**: A measure of the profitability of an investment, calculated by dividing the net profit (or loss) generated by the investment by the initial cost of the investment and expressing the result as a percentage.

179) **Risk Management**: The process of identifying, assessing, and mitigating risks to an organization's capital and earnings.

180) **Risk Parity**: An investment strategy that allocates capital across different asset classes based on their risk contributions rather than their market capitalizations or historical returns. Risk parity portfolios seek to achieve balanced risk exposure and stable returns across various market conditions.

181) **Risk-Adjusted Return**: A measure of investment performance that considers the level of risk taken to achieve a certain level of return. Risk-adjusted return metrics, such as the Sharpe ratio or the Treynor ratio, help investors evaluate the efficiency of investment portfolios and compare alternative investments.

182) **Risk-Free Asset**: An asset with a guaranteed return and no risk of loss, typically represented by short-term government securities, such as Treasury bills or bonds. Risk-free assets serve as a benchmark for evaluating the performance of other investments and are used in various financial calculations, such as the capital asset pricing model (CAPM).

183) **Risk-Free Rate**: The theoretical rate of return on an investment with zero risk of financial loss, typically represented by the yield on government securities such as Treasury bills or bonds. The risk-free rate serves as a benchmark for assessing the relative risk and return of other investments.

184) **Rollover IRA**: An individual retirement account (IRA) that allows individuals to transfer or "rollover" funds from a qualified retirement plan, such as a 401(k), into a tax-advantaged account without incurring taxes or penalties.

185) **Secondary Market**: A financial market where existing securities are bought and sold among investors, rather than directly from the issuer. Secondary markets provide liquidity for investors to trade securities after their initial issuance and determine their market prices based on supply and demand dynamics.

186) **Securities Clearing**: The process of settling and reconciling financial transactions involving securities, ensuring that securities are transferred from sellers to buyers and funds are transferred from buyers to sellers, typically facilitated by a clearinghouse or central depository.

187) **Securities Exchange Commission (SEC)**: A U.S. government agency responsible for regulating securities markets and protecting investors, overseeing stock exchanges, securities brokers, and investment advisors.

188) **Securities Exchange Commission (SEC)**: The U.S. government agency responsible for regulating and overseeing the securities industry, including securities exchanges, brokerage firms, investment advisers, and publicly traded companies. The SEC enforces securities laws, promotes market transparency, and protects investors from fraud and misconduct.

189) **Securities Exchange**: A regulated marketplace where securities such as stocks, bonds, and derivatives are bought and sold. Examples include stock exchanges like the New York Stock Exchange (NYSE) and electronic trading platforms like NASDAQ.

190) **Securities Fraud**: Illegal activities involving the manipulation, misrepresentation, or false disclosure of information related to securities or financial instruments, aimed at deceiving investors for financial gain.

191) **Securities Fraud**: Illegal activities involving the manipulation, misrepresentation, or false disclosure of information related to securities or financial instruments, aimed at deceiving investors for financial gain. Securities fraud can take various forms, including insider trading, accounting fraud, market manipulation, and Ponzi schemes.

192) **Securities Lending**: The practice of temporarily transferring securities from one party (the lender) to another (the borrower) in exchange for a fee, typically used by institutional investors and broker-dealers to generate additional income.

193) **Securities Lending**: The practice of temporarily transferring securities from one party (the lender) to another party (the borrower) in exchange for a fee or collateral, with the borrower agreeing to return the securities at a later date. Securities lending allows investors to earn additional income on their portfolios and provides liquidity to short sellers and market participants.

194) **Securitization**: The process of pooling together various types of debt (such as mortgages, auto loans, or credit card debt) and selling them as securities to investors.

195) **Short Selling**: A trading strategy in which an investor borrows shares of stock from a broker and sells them on the open market with the expectation that the stock price will decline. The investor later buys back the shares at a lower price to return them to the broker, profiting from the difference in price.

196) **Solvency**: The financial condition of an individual, company, or institution indicating its ability to meet long-term financial obligations. It is often assessed by comparing total assets to total liabilities.

197) **Sovereign Wealth Fund**: A state-owned investment fund that invests in various financial assets, such as stocks, bonds, real estate, and infrastructure projects, typically with the goal of generating long-term wealth for a country's citizens.

198) **Speculation**: The act of buying, selling, or trading financial assets with the expectation of profiting from short-term price movements or market fluctuations, rather than from the underlying fundamentals or intrinsic value of the assets. Speculation involves higher risks and may result in substantial gains or losses.

199) **Stagflation**: An economic phenomenon characterized by simultaneous high inflation and stagnant economic growth, often accompanied by high unemployment and low consumer spending. Stagflation presents challenges for monetary policymakers, as traditional policy tools may be ineffective in addressing both inflation and economic stagnation.

200) **Stochastic Process**: A random process that evolves over time according to probabilistic rules, commonly used in option pricing models and risk management.

201) **Stock Buyback**: A corporate action in which a company repurchases its own shares from the open market, reducing the number of outstanding shares and increasing the ownership stake of remaining shareholders. Stock buybacks are often used to return capital to shareholders, boost earnings per share, or signal confidence in the company's prospects.

202) **Stock Options**: Derivative contracts that give the holder the right, but not the obligation, to buy or sell a specific amount of a stock at a predetermined price within a specified time frame.

203) **Stock Split**: A corporate action in which a company divides its existing shares into multiple shares, effectively increasing the number of outstanding shares while reducing the price per share. Stock splits do not change the total market value of the company but may improve liquidity and make shares more affordable to investors.

204) **Stress Testing**: A risk management technique used to assess the resilience of financial institutions or portfolios to adverse economic scenarios, typically involving simulated shocks to key risk factors.

205) **Structured Finance**: A financial technique that involves pooling together various financial assets, such as loans, mortgages, or receivables, and creating structured securities with different risk profiles and cash flow characteristics. Structured finance techniques are used to securitize assets and transfer risk to investors.

206) **Structured Investment Vehicle (SIV)**: A special-purpose entity created to invest in a portfolio of long-term assets, such as mortgage-backed securities or collateralized debt obligations, funded by issuing short-term debt securities in the commercial paper market. SIVs use leverage to enhance returns but can be vulnerable to liquidity and credit risks.

207) **Structured Product**: A complex financial instrument created by combining multiple securities or derivatives to provide customized risk-return profiles or exposure to specific market factors.

208) **Systematic Risk**: The risk that is inherent to the entire market or an entire market segment, affecting the overall economy and all securities within it, as opposed to specific risk that only affects individual assets or sectors.

209) **Systemic Risk**: The risk of widespread financial instability or collapse within an entire financial system, often resulting from interconnectedness and contagion effects among financial institutions and markets.

210) **Tax-Loss Harvesting**: An investment strategy that involves selling securities at a loss to offset capital gains and reduce tax liabilities in a taxable investment portfolio. Tax-loss harvesting allows investors to realize losses on underperforming investments while maintaining exposure to the market and potentially improving after-tax returns.

211) **Technical Analysis**: A method of analyzing securities and financial markets based on historical price and volume data to forecast future price movements. Technical analysts use charts, patterns, and indicators to identify trends, support and resistance levels, and potential entry and exit points for trading.

212) **Time Value of Money (TVM)**: The principle that money available at the present time is worth more than the same amount in the future due to its potential earning capacity. TVM is fundamental to various financial calculations such as present value, future value, and net present value.

213) **Treasury Inflation-Protected Securities (TIPS)**: Bonds issued by the U.S. Department of the Treasury that offer protection against inflation by adjusting their principal value based on changes in the Consumer Price Index (CPI). TIPS provide investors with a hedge against purchasing power erosion caused by inflation and pay semiannual interest based on the inflation-adjusted principal amount.

214) **Underwater Mortgage**: A mortgage loan in which the outstanding loan balance exceeds the current market value of the underlying property, resulting in negative equity for the homeowner. Underwater mortgages pose financial challenges for homeowners and may lead to foreclosure or strategic default.

215) **Underwater Option**: An options contract in which the current market price of the underlying asset is below the strike price for call options or above the strike price for put options. Underwater options have no intrinsic value and are unlikely to be exercised profitably at expiration.

216) **Underwriting**: The process by which investment banks or insurance companies assess and assume financial risk on behalf of clients, typically in relation to new securities offerings, insurance policies, or loan agreements. Underwriters evaluate the risk and determine the terms and pricing of the transaction.

217) **Value at Risk (VaR)**: A statistical measure of the maximum potential loss that a portfolio or investment may incur over a specified time horizon and confidence level. VaR is used to quantify and manage the risk of investment portfolios and assess the adequacy of capital reserves.

218) **Value Investing**: An investment strategy that focuses on purchasing undervalued stocks or assets trading below their intrinsic value, as determined by fundamental analysis of financial metrics, earnings potential, and business prospects. Value investors seek to buy assets with a margin of safety and hold them for the long term to realize capital appreciation.

219) **Variance Swap**: A financial derivative contract that allows investors to speculate on or hedge against changes in the volatility of an underlying asset, such as a stock index or currency pair. Variance swaps pay off based on the difference between realized and implied volatility levels over a specified period.

220) **Venture Capital (VC)**: Equity financing provided to early-stage or growth-stage companies with high growth potential, typically in exchange for an ownership stake in the company. Venture capital investors often take an active role in supporting the growth and development of portfolio companies and seek to realize returns through a successful exit, such as an initial public offering (IPO) or acquisition.

221) **Vesting**: The process by which an employee earns ownership rights or entitlements to employer-provided benefits, such as stock options, retirement contributions, or employer-matching funds, over time. Vesting schedules specify the time period or conditions under which these benefits become fully owned by the employee.

222) **Volatility Smile**: A graphical representation of the implied volatility of options at different strike prices and expiration dates, often showing a smile-shaped curve indicating that out-of-the-money options have higher implied volatility than at-the-money options.

223) **Volatility**: A measure of the variation in the price of a financial instrument over time.

224) **Warrant**: A financial instrument that gives the holder the right, but not the obligation, to buy a specific quantity of underlying securities, such as common stock, at a predetermined price within a specified time frame. Warrants are often issued as part of a bond or preferred stock offering and provide additional upside potential to investors.

225) **Weighted Average Cost of Capital (WACC)**: A financial metric that represents the average cost of capital for a company, calculated by weighting the cost of equity, debt, and other sources of financing based on their respective proportions in the company's capital structure. WACC is used to discount cash flows and evaluate investment opportunities.

226) **Wholesale Banking**: Banking services provided to large corporate clients, institutional investors, and other financial institutions, typically involving complex financial products, structured financing, and advisory services. Wholesale banking activities include corporate lending, trade finance, capital markets, and treasury services.

227) **Working Capital**: A financial metric that represents the difference between a company's current assets and current liabilities, reflecting its ability to meet short-term obligations and fund day-to-day operations. Working capital management is crucial for maintaining liquidity, managing cash flow, and supporting business growth.

228) **Working Capital**: The difference between a company's current assets and current liabilities, representing the amount of capital available to fund day-to-day operations and short-term financial obligations. Positive working capital indicates that a company has sufficient liquidity to cover its short-term liabilities, while negative working capital may signal financial distress.

229) **XIRR (Extended Internal Rate of Return)**: A financial metric used to calculate the annualized rate of return for an investment with irregular cash flows and multiple investment or withdrawal dates. XIRR accounts for the timing and magnitude of cash flows and is commonly used to evaluate the performance of investment portfolios.

230) **XIRR (Extended Internal Rate of Return)**: A financial metric used to calculate the annualized rate of return for an investment with irregular cash flows and multiple investment or withdrawal dates. XIRR accounts for the timing and magnitude of cash flows and is commonly used to evaluate the performance of investment portfolios.

231) **Yield Curve Inversion**: A phenomenon that occurs when the yields on short-term bonds exceed the yields on long-term bonds. It is often considered a signal of an impending economic downturn or recession.

232) **Yield Curve Steepening**: A change in the shape of the yield curve characterized by an increase in the yield spread between short-term and long-term interest rates. Yield curve steepening often occurs during periods of economic expansion or inflationary pressures and may signal expectations of future interest rate hikes by central banks.

233) **Yield Curve**: A graphical representation of interest rates for bonds of similar credit quality but different maturities, plotted against their respective maturity dates. The yield curve provides insights into market expectations for future interest rates and economic conditions, with upward-sloping, flat, and inverted yield curves indicating different market scenarios.

234) **Yield Spread**: The difference between the yields of two different fixed-income securities or financial instruments, typically expressed in basis points (bps) or percentage points. Yield spreads are used to compare the relative risk and return of bonds, loans, or credit instruments with similar maturities but different credit ratings or characteristics.

235) **Yield**: The income return on an investment, usually expressed as a percentage of the asset's price or face value.

236) **Zero Coupon Bond**: A type of bond that pays no periodic interest payments to the bondholder but is instead sold at a discount to its face value and redeemed at full face value at maturity, providing a return through capital appreciation.

237) **Zero-Sum Game**: A situation in which one participant's gain is exactly balanced by another participant's loss, resulting in a net-zero outcome. In financial markets, trading is often viewed as a zero-sum game, as gains made by one investor come at the expense of losses incurred by another investor.

238) **Zero-Sum Game**: A situation in which one participant's gain is exactly balanced by another participant's loss, resulting in a net-zero outcome. Zero-sum games are common in competitive situations, such as trading, gambling, and strategic interactions, where one party's success comes at the expense of another party's failure.

239) **Zero-Sum Game**: A situation in which one participant's gain is exactly balanced by another participant's loss, resulting in a net-zero outcome. Zero-sum games are common in competitive situations, such as trading, gambling, and strategic interactions, where one party's success comes at the expense of another party's failure.

240) **Z-Score**: A statistical measure used to evaluate the financial health and creditworthiness of a company, calculated based on various financial ratios and indicators such as profitability, leverage, liquidity, and solvency. Z-scores are used by investors, creditors, and analysts to assess the risk of corporate bankruptcy or financial distress.